THE BUSH PILOTS

TIME LIFE ®
BOOKS

Other Publications:
PLANET EARTH
COLLECTOR'S LIBRARY OF THE CIVIL WAR
LIBRARY OF HEALTH
CLASSICS OF THE OLD WEST
THE GOOD COOK
THE SEAFARERS
THE ENCYCLOPEDIA OF COLLECTIBLES
THE GREAT CITIES
WORLD WAR II
HOME REPAIR AND IMPROVEMENT
THE WORLD'S WILD PLACES
THE TIME-LIFE LIBRARY OF BOATING
HUMAN BEHAVIOR
THE ART OF SEWING
THE OLD WEST
THE EMERGENCE OF MAN
THE AMERICAN WILDERNESS
THE TIME-LIFE ENCYCLOPEDIA OF GARDENING
LIFE LIBRARY OF PHOTOGRAPHY
THIS FABULOUS CENTURY
FOODS OF THE WORLD
TIME-LIFE LIBRARY OF AMERICA
TIME-LIFE LIBRARY OF ART
GREAT AGES OF MAN
LIFE SCIENCE LIBRARY
THE LIFE HISTORY OF THE UNITED STATES
TIME READING PROGRAM
LIFE NATURE LIBRARY
LIFE WORLD LIBRARY

FAMILY LIBRARY:
HOW THINGS WORK IN YOUR HOME
THE TIME-LIFE BOOK OF THE FAMILY CAR
THE TIME-LIFE FAMILY LEGAL GUIDE
THE TIME-LIFE BOOK OF FAMILY FINANCE

This volume is one of a series that traces the adventure and science of aviation, from the earliest manned balloon ascension through the era of jet flight.

THE BUSH PILOTS

BY THE EDITORS OF TIME-LIFE BOOKS

TIME-LIFE BOOKS, ALEXANDRIA, VIRGINIA

Time-Life Books Inc.
is a wholly owned subsidiary of

TIME INCORPORATED

FOUNDER: Henry R. Luce 1898-1967

Editor-in-Chief: Henry Anatole Grunwald
President: J. Richard Munro
Chairman of the Board: Ralph P. Davidson
Executive Vice President: Clifford J. Grum
Editorial Director: Ralph Graves
Group Vice President, Books: Joan D. Manley
Vice Chairman: Arthur Temple

TIME-LIFE BOOKS INC.

EDITOR: George Constable
Executive Editor: George Daniels
Director of Design: Louis Klein
Board of Editors: Dale M. Brown, Thomas H. Flaherty Jr.,
Thomas A. Lewis, Martin Mann, Robert G. Mason,
John Paul Porter, Gerry Schremp, Gerald Simons,
Rosalind Stubenberg, Kit van Tulleken
Director of Administration: David L. Harrison
Director of Research: Carolyn L. Sackett
Director of Photography: Richard Kenin

PRESIDENT: Carl G. Jaeger
Executive Vice Presidents: John Steven Maxwell,
David J. Walsh
Vice Presidents: George Artandi, Stephen L. Bair,
Peter G. Barnes, Nicholas Benton, John L. Canova,
Beatrice T. Dobie, James L. Mercer, Paul R. Stewart

THE EPIC OF FLIGHT

EDITOR: Dale M. Brown
Designer: Albert Sherman
Chief Researcher: W. Mark Hamilton

Editorial Staff for *The Bush Pilots*

Associate Editors: Lee Hassig,
David S. Thomson (text); Robin Richman (pictures)
Staff Writers: Allan Fallow, Adrianne Goodman,
Glenn Martin McNatt, John Manners
Researchers: Betty Ajemian, Barbara Brownell,
Anne Munoz-Furlong, B. Jean Strong
Assistant Designer: Anne K. DuVivier
Copy Coordinators: Stephen G. Hyslop, Anthony K. Pordes
Picture Coordinator: Betsy Donahue
Editorial Assistants: Caroline A. Boubin,
Constance B. Strawbridge

Editorial Operations
Design: Arnold C. Holeywell (assistant director);
Anne B. Landry (art coordinator);
James J. Cox (quality control)
Research: Phyllis K. Wise (assistant director),
Louise D. Forstall
Copy Room: Susan Galloway Goldberg (director),
Celia Beattie, Ricki Tarlow
Production: Feliciano Madrid (director), Gordon E. Buck,
Peter Inchauteguiz

Correspondents: Elisabeth Kraemer (Bonn); Margot
Hapgood, Dorothy Bacon (London); Miriam Hsia, Lucy T.
Voulgaris (New York); Maria Vincenza Aloisi, Josephine du
Brusle (Paris); Ann Natanson (Rome). Valuable assistance
was also provided by: John Dunn (Melbourne); Ernest
Shirley (Mudgeeraba, Queensland); Christina Lieberman,
Cornelis Verwaal (New York); John Scott (Ottawa); Peter
Argo (Perth); Ed Ogle (Vancouver).

THE CONSULTANTS

R.E.G. Davies, a noted aviation historian, has
flown with bush pilots in Alaska, Borneo, Colombia, Nepal and New Guinea. A Fellow of
the Royal Aeronautical Society, he is the
author of *Airlines of the United States since
1914, Airlines of Latin America since 1919*
and *A History of the World's Airlines.* In 1982
he served as the Lindbergh Professor of
Aerospace History at the National Air and
Space Museum in Washington, D.C.

Kenneth M. Molson, who obtained his pilot's
license in 1936, attended McGill University in
Montreal and the Boeing School of Aeronautics in Oakland, California. From 1960 to
1967 he served as Curator of the National
Aviation Museum in Ottawa. He is the author
of *Pioneering in Canadian Air Transport* and
co-author of *Canadian Aircraft since 1909.*

Terry Gwynn-Jones, who reviewed and contributed to Chapters 2 and 3, on Australia
and New Guinea, joined Britain's Royal Air
Force in 1951 and later served with the
Royal Canadian Air Force and the Royal
Australian Air Force. In 1975 he set an
around-the-world speed record—122 hours
and 17 minutes—for piston-engined aircraft.
His books include *True Australian Air Stories*
and *Heroic Australian Air Stories.*

For information about any Time-Life book, please write:
Reader Information
Time-Life Books
541 North Fairbanks Court
Chicago, Illinois 60611

Library of Congress Cataloguing in Publication Data
The bush pilots.
(The Epic of flight)
Bibliography: p.
Includes index.
1. Bush pilots. I. Time-Life Books. II. Title.
III. Series.
TL711.L7S43 1983   387.7'4   82-19155
ISBN 0-8094-3312-5
ISBN 0-8094-3309-5 (lib. bdg.)

CONTENTS

In Anchorage after a 1934 fur-buying trip, charter pilot Art Woodley (right) and buyer James Kennedy display their cargo of pelts on Woodley's plane.

Master aviators of the wilderness

One day in 1932, pilot Bob Reeve, ferrying supplies to a remote Alaskan mining town, landed at his destination to find a grizzled miner eagerly awaiting his arrival. "Got my snoose?" asked the oldtimer.

It took Reeve a moment to recall that on his last trip he had promised to bring some snuff, a seemingly trivial request he had promptly forgotten. To his chagrin, the miner ignored his apologies and stalked off to proclaim that Reeve was "no good"—teaching the pilot a humiliating lesson in bush-flying etiquette: Always honor a promise.

In sparsely populated areas around the globe, where a packet of needles or a pouch of tobacco was regarded as a luxury beyond compare, bush pilots like Reeve were a life line to the outside. And the farther they flew from civilization, the more they were appreciated. Mexican mine operators hired them to wing silver and gold past the bandits who lurked along the mountain trails traversed by slow mule train. Eskimos scrawled messages to friends in distant villages on the flimsy fuselages of bush planes. And in the barren Australian Outback, the citizens of one tiny town gathered to sweep the pebbles off an improvised airstrip so that a flier could make a smooth landing.

Trappers and prospectors, missionaries and mountaineers, sportsmen and entrepreneurs in the most remote corners of the world during the first half of the century all came to share one thing—their reliance on the bush pilots.

A wilderness tent serves as a distribution point for the freight tiny Western Canada Airways ferried to the Red Lake gold fields in 1927.

An off-duty New Guinea flier rests at one of his company's bush outposts—a combination passenger terminal, freight depot and pilots' quarters.

A Mexican guard watches over a stack of silver ingots about to be loaded on a Lockheed Vega. The plane, a favorite among bush pilots, was used by the San Luis Mining Company to transport the bullion safely out of the Sierra Madre.

In 1929, a party of Juneau businessmen shows off their catch after a day's fishing trip to Alaska's Lake Hasselborg—a half-hour hop from the city in this pontoon-equipped Lockheed Vega piloted by Floyd Keadle (third from right behind the engine).

New and old means of transport meet in the arid Australian Outback sometime in the early 1920s. Camels, which had been imported from Asia in the

late 19th Century to serve as pack animals, soon gave way to planes such as this World War I-surplus Avro 504.

In the Ecuadorian jungle, an Atshuara Indian watches missionary pilot Hobey Lawrence report his safe landing in potentially hostile territory.

1

A wild northern breed

We flew, said Noel Wien, the greatest of Alaska's early bush pilots, "without a radio and without weather reports over unmapped mountains in the worst weather that God inflicts on this earth."

Wien's succinct catalogue of the perils he and his fellow bush pilots faced in Alaska could be matched in degree, if not in detail, by those encountered in any of the globe's other wilderness areas where this rare breed of aviators took root. A tough, independent lot, these pilots pioneered the use of airplanes to carry people and goods to places that had been accessible only on horseback, or by oxcart, dog sled or canoe.

They flew small secondhand planes that had been through so many minor crashes and subsequent repairs that, as one pilot cheerfully admitted, they were little more than "collections of spare parts." In these slow, much-patched craft the intrepid aviators not only flew over the ice-cloaked mountains and endless tundra of Alaska, but also penetrated the forbidding Barrens of northern Canada, the scorched Outback of Australia, the humid jungles of New Guinea, the razor-backed ridges of Mexico's Sierra Madre and the tangled rain forests of the Amazon.

The bush pilots and their planes, in effect, yanked these isolated places into the 20th Century. Flying in minutes or hours over territory so rugged that it took days or weeks to traverse on the ground, they connected countless remote settlements and lone individuals with the outside world, bringing in medicines, mail, essential commodities and emergency aid. Entire cultures that had yet to enjoy overland transportation by railroad or highway leapfrogged straight into the air age.

Bush flying began after World War I, when there was a glut of surplus warplanes and service-trained pilots. Some of these young men remained so smitten with flying that they found a new use for their skills: inaugurating air services in the more remote corners of the globe. The word "bush," customarily used to describe the scrublands in the interior of South Africa, came to include all of the wilderness areas—from treeless tundra to desert dunes—over which these aviators flew.

To reach such inhospitable areas, bush pilots were forced to develop flying techniques undreamed of by aviators in the more civilized parts of the world. With few airports available, they learned to set planes down on sand bars in the middle of rivers, in swampy jungle clearings, on narrow strips perched precariously on the sides of mountains, or on arctic ice floes. They learned, when a faltering engine made a jungle

Harold Gillam, one of Alaska's first bush pilots, gazes coolly from the open cockpit of a Waco biplane. His fame for flying in stormy weather and treating his passengers to minor crack-ups prompted a third-grade Indian admirer to write: "He thrill em, Chill em, Spill em, But no killem Gillam."

crash inevitable, to aim between the trees, shearing off the plane's wings but saving themselves and their passengers.

The extraordinarily dangerous flying performed by these aviators made them larger-than-life folk heroes to the people in the regions where they flew. Stories of the bush pilots' skill and often foolhardy courage grew and multiplied—and eventually penetrated beyond their own wilderness regions. Newspapers in the 1920s and 1930s reported their more remarkable triumphs—and avidly followed the desperate aerial manhunts that developed when one of the fliers was forced down in some unmapped, Godforsaken wilderness. From all these tales and newspaper stories grew a body of lore as dramatic as the heart-stopping legends of air combat produced by the two World Wars, and containing examples of flying skill and dogged determination unmatched since the invention of the airplane.

The great advances in aviation brought by World War II did not kill bush flying. Rather, it spread in the War's wake, the pilots using airfields left behind by the combatants and entering areas little known before. Improved technology brought better aircraft, more reliable communications gear and sophisticated navigational aids. In Australia and North America, two cradles of bush flying, some of the pioneer air charter services begun between the Wars grew into full-fledged, even international, airlines, among them Alaskan Airways, Canadian Pacific Airlines and Australia's Qantas. But true bush flying continued in wild places no airline will ever reach—still a solitary profession peculiar to loners who thrived on wresting a living from flying despite extremes of hardship.

It was in Canada, by the narrowest of margins, that bush flying began. Soon after the 1918 Armistice, a Canadian forester named Ellwood Wilson, employed in the great forests of Quebec Province by the Laurentide Company, realized that airplanes offered an excellent method both of spotting forest fires and of mapping the huge forested areas owned by Laurentide and other papermakers. Early in 1919, when Wilson found out that the U.S. Navy was giving Canada several war-surplus Curtiss HS-2L coastal patrol flying boats, he asked for two on loan. Wilson then hired Captain Stuart Graham, just returning from piloting with the Royal Naval Air Service, to fly the planes. The Curtisses were awkward contraptions resembling pelicans, with their two wings mounted high on tub-shaped fuselages. In rough conditions a pilot needed the help of the engineer to manhandle the controls. To maneuver the plane on water, the hard-pressed engineer was often forced to climb out on the lower wing, using his weight to dip the right or left wing-tip floats into the water and thus help the plane pivot in a right or left turn. Despite these drawbacks, HS-2Ls would become the standard early bush planes in Canada. They were large enough to carry a good load and they could put down on almost any lake or river—of which Canada's wilderness areas had an endless supply.

Graham and his engineer, Walter Kahre, managed to deliver the first

The world's first bush-flying operation begins in June of 1919 as a Curtiss HS-2L flying boat is eased into the water in Halifax, Nova Scotia. After testing the cumbersome craft for a couple of days, pilot Stuart Graham flew it into the Canadian wilderness, where it was used to chart timberlands and patrol for fires.

HS-2L to Lac à la Tortue, the forest patrol's home base, on June 8. The trip had taken four days and had covered 645 miles—the longest cross-country flight made in Canada up to that time. Graham then picked up the second HS-2L and flew that one to Lac à la Tortue as well.

Equipped with its pair of awkward aircraft, the forest patrol got off to a modest start in the summer of 1919, scouting fires and taking aerial photographs of the huge timbered areas in Quebec Province's rugged St. Maurice River valley. Graham and Kahre continued this demanding work for two more seasons, but the expenses proved so high that the Laurentide Company finally balked at underwriting the operation. In late 1921, in an effort to make the forest patrol self-sustaining, it was reorganized as the Laurentide Air Services Ltd., a separate company, with an energetic former Royal Air Force instructor and barnstormer named William Roy Maxwell as the vice president.

Charged with finding additional financial backers, Maxwell swiftly located a patron in wealthy Quebec shipbuilder Thomas Hall, who bankrolled Laurentide Air Services to the tune of $10,000 and turned it into a commercial operation. In the summer of 1922—the flying boats could not operate when winter froze Canada's waterways—Laurentide's planes flew 688 hours and carried 310 paying customers, becoming one of the world's first bush charter services.

Business looked so promising that Maxwell bought a dozen or so more surplus HS-2Ls—most still in their original crates—and hired a half-dozen additional pilots. This let the company extend its range and map 20,000 square miles of timberland in the neighboring province of Ontario, surveying in 160 hours of flying time an area so huge that ground surveyors would have needed five or six years to cover it.

21

The startling success of this venture carried within it the seeds of Laurentide's doom. The Ontario government was so impressed that it soon began its own Ontario Provincial Air Service, or OPAS, luring Roy Maxwell and other key personnel from Laurentide, and a good part of its business. The OPAS pilots worked hard, horsing their clumsy HS-2Ls over the length and breadth of Ontario. In 1924 they flew almost 2,600 hours, much of it on fire patrol, though they also did aerial surveys, identifying which areas held prime timber, which had less valuable stands of trees and which had been burned over by fires. Later they added a more dangerous sort of work, airlifting fire fighters into blazing forests, often landing on tiny lakes obscured by smoke to take men, pumps, hoses and other equipment as close as possible to the rampaging blazes. In 1926 OPAS further proved the value of airplanes in the bush by ferrying 27 men and 6,420 pounds of gear to fight a fire that, Maxwell reported, could not have been reached and extinguished in any other way. "No man," he said, "approached it or left it by ground."

The records of OPAS indicate that the hard-worked pilots also played hard, especially during the long winters, when flying was curtailed. That drink and women were seldom far from the fliers' minds after work is clearly implied by the minutes of a mock court-martial. The accused was a young pilot who, in December 1925, had allegedly committed the hideous crime of wearing his dashing flying costume plus helmet and goggles into several bars in OPAS' headquarters town of Sault Ste. Marie with the express purpose of soliciting "advances by the fair sex."

An HS-2L of the pioneering Laurentide Air Services gets ready to take off with a party of hunters from Haileybury, Ontario. Laurentide's regular passenger flights over the Canadian wilderness, beginning in 1924, constituted the first scheduled air service in Canada.

A crated HS-2L arrives early in 1924 at Lac à la Tortue, Quebec. There the craft was assembled for delivery to the newly formed Ontario Provincial Air Service. Laurentide sold a fleet of HS-2Ls to OPAS, which, backed by the Ontario government, soon put the older company out of business.

The prisoner explained to the "judge," a pilot named J. R. "Rod" Ross, and a convocation of other fellow aviators that he had simply put on the leather flying helmet for warmth and that the goggles, of course, had been attached to it. When the court suggested that he had worn his flying rig while off duty because he was drunk, the accused claimed that he had had only one drink in his life. At this the courtroom exploded with shouts of, "That's what's the matter with him!" After the guilty verdict Judge Ross pronounced the dread sentence: Banishment from the Boiler Room, a Sault Ste. Marie bar, for two weeks.

Despite its pilots' penchant for revelry, OPAS, funded by the Ontario government, was able to operate successfully into the 1940s. Laurentide, which had lost both business and key personnel to OPAS, was no longer profitable. Early in 1925, the world's pioneer bush-flying outfit went out of business.

Had Laurentide been able to stay afloat just a few months longer, it might have been saved by one of the biggest gold rushes in Canadian history, the great Red Lake find of 1925, which spawned several new bush services. One of these new outfits, Patricia Airways and Exploration, Ltd., was formed by a threesome of investors who purchased a Curtiss Lark biplane. The company's principal pilot was Captain Harold A. "Doc" Oaks, a Royal Flying Corps veteran as well as a geologist and mining engineer who had already mushed by dog sled into the Red Lake fields. He had staked a claim, but then, deciding that surer money could be made flying others to the digs, leaped at the opportunity to fly

Part of OPAS' fleet of HS-2Ls and a single D.H.61 stand before a boldly emblazoned hangar at the organization's Sault Ste. Marie headquarters. By the mid-1920s, OPAS was one of the largest bush-flying operations in the world, surveying timberland and spotting and fighting fires for the Ontario government.

for Patricia Airways. He sold his claim and began taking passengers in to Red Lake in April 1926 in a leased HS-2L and a tiny Curtiss Lark biplane with two open cockpits, one for the pilot, the other roomy enough to carry 400 pounds of mining equipment or a pair of prospectors in cramped discomfort. Through most of 1926 and into 1927, using floats in summer and newly developed airplane skis during the snowy months, Oaks made as many as 10 flights a day in the Lark, shuttling 260 passengers to Red Lake—along with 14,000 pounds of prospecting and mining gear and 3,000 pounds of mail.

The profits racked up by this shoestring operation—the Lark was far less expensive to operate than Laurentide's fleet of heavy HS-2Ls—prompted Oaks to strike out on his own. He went to see James A. Richardson, a wealthy Winnipeg grain merchant, who agreed to invest in a new air service. They baptized the creation Western Canada Airways, Ltd., an imposing name for an operation that at first consisted of only one plane. Doc Oaks was both the pilot and the company's manager, Al Cheesman was the sole mechanic, and a man named J. A. MacDougall acted as clerk. Oaks once more found himself in the tiring business of ferrying prospectors and freight from a lake at Gold Pines, Ontario, to various mining camps.

Soon, however, Oaks's reputation as an able aviator and hard-working organizer gained the fledgling outfit a contract from the Canadian government for a major freight-hauling job. It was an adventurous undertaking, and it put Western Canada Airways into the record books. The government was eager to extend a railway from central Manitoba to Hudson Bay as a route for shipping wheat from Canada's midwestern prairies to Europe. Fort Churchill or Port Nelson, both in northern

On the shore of Ontario's Red Lake, Harold A. "Doc" Oaks, owner and sole operator of Patricia Airways and Exploration, Ltd., stands beside the firm's Curtiss Lark, equipped with a single broad float. Patricia Airways was named for the northwestern Ontario district in which the Red Lake gold fields were located.

Manitoba and free of ice in summer, might be suitable as a rail terminus if the bottom of Hudson Bay at either town could be dredged deeper to accommodate the big grain ships. Drilling would have to be done to determine whether the bottom was sand or rock—and the work would have to be completed soon, before the track-laying gangs got to Hudson Bay during the next summer.

That was where Doc Oaks and Western Canada Airways came in. If they could fly the machinery to Hudson Bay, drilling could start at once. Oaks was interested in the proposal—despite his awareness of what the flying weather would be like that far north in winter. With Richardson's backing he acquired three Fokker Universals, rugged single-engined, high-winged monoplanes with commodious cabins for freight.

To help fly the Fokkers, Oaks lured a pair of experienced Canadian bush pilots from OPAS, RFC veterans Frederick "Steve" Stevenson and Rod Ross. They were joined by a Norwegian named Bernt Balchen, who was already known as a cold-weather flier. He had participated in a much-publicized arctic air search in 1925 for two lost explorers, the Norwegian Roald Amundsen and the American Lincoln Ellsworth.

Balchen, who kept a diary, recorded with amusement his first sight of Western Canada's headquarters in Hudson, Ontario. It was "little more than a lean-to," he noted, but it had "an impressive sign over the door, 'Western Canada Airways.' " This turned out to be the air service's administration building and included "ticket office,

One of Canada's countless watery landing strips stretches to the horizon in this pilot's-eye view from a Dominion Airways Fairchild in 1936.

freight station and passenger terminal for the whole flying gold rush.''

The Fokkers having arrived from the United States, Stevenson and Balchen took off from Hudson on March 23, 1927, with Rod Ross and Al Cheesman acting as engineers—a term bush pilots used to describe their mechanics. They picked up an initial installment of 1,200 pounds of drilling equipment at an airstrip near Cache Lake, which was at the end of the rail line, and then zoomed off again, bound for Fort Churchill, where the initial drilling would take place.

The first several flights were uneventful, but on one return trip from Fort Churchill to Cache Lake, a grueling 125-mile haul over a bleak, snow-covered wilderness, Stevenson experienced the sort of unpleasant adventure that virtually all early bush pilots of the North Country, flying through subfreezing weather in the open cockpits of the era's mechanically unpredictable aircraft, would encounter sooner or later. Balchen and Cheesman made the flight back to Cache Lake safely enough, but Stevenson, flying alone so that Rod Ross could stay behind to oversee operations at Fort Churchill, failed to show up. All had been well until he was some 75 miles north of Cache Lake. Then the main oil pipe to his Fokker's Wright Whirlwind engine ruptured. Despite the spewing oil, he put the Fokker down on a small frozen lake in the wilderness. Having seen no sign of human habitation anywhere near the spot, Stevenson did the only sensible thing. With the early dark of a far northern winter's evening descending swiftly, he wrapped his fur flying gear more tightly about him and bedded down for the

The Western Canada Airways team of Rod Ross, Bernt Balchen, Al Cheesman and Fred Stevenson stand before a Fokker Universal in 1927. The line had just completed the first large airlift in the far north, taking eight tons of gear and 14 surveyors and engineers from Manitoba to Hudson Bay.

A drill flown in section by section by Western Canada Airways pierces the ice to take soil samples from the bottom of Hudson Bay near Churchill, Manitoba. The wagon parked behind the drilling apparatus carried the engine that was used to power the drill bit.

night in the plane's cabin while both wind and wolves howled outside.

With first light the next morning, Stevenson began exploring and found fresh tracks, which he followed to an Indian's cabin. There he arranged to hire a dog sled and mushed southward, but the Indian's dogs were in poor condition and soon gave up, exhausted. Stevenson then started walking, slogging laboriously through hip-high drifts.

Balchen and Cheesman were also busy at first light, taking off in their Fokker and flying northward. They soon caught a glimpse of Stevenson's downed plane and also landed on the lake, but found no trace of their fellow aviator. Planes were precious commodities, though, and they decided to fly the downed Fokker out. Cheesman, who had had some pilot training, somehow got its engine going and took off without realizing that the oil line was broken. Noticing a drop in oil pressure, he swiftly put the lumbering craft back on the ground, fixed the broken line and took off once more. This time he succeeded in flying the aircraft back to Cache Lake, Balchen following in the other Fokker.

When Stevenson finally appeared, having trudged for three days through snowdrifts, the first thing he saw was his abandoned airplane, already sitting on the Cache Lake strip waiting for him. Stevenson's troubles were not quite over. During a subsequent takeoff from Cache Lake he damaged his undercarriage. To have the broken parts fixed, he was forced to transport them 136 miles to the nearest railroad repair shop. The journey was made in an open-air railroad handcar, with Cheesman pumping on one handle and him the other.

Despite such trials and tribulations, the four aviators completed hauling eight tons of gear and 14 workmen to Fort Churchill by April 22, finishing their mission just as the spring thaw was setting in. Balchen recalled that when they roared off on their last trip, the melting ice on Cache Lake was so covered with water that the ski-equipped Fokkers looked like seaplanes getting airborne.

The Canadian government was impressed. This had been the first large airlift in Canada and one of the first in the world, with some individual items weighing more than 650 pounds and a few crates measuring more than 20 feet in length. "There has been no more brilliant operation in the history of commercial flying," noted the otherwise understated government report on civil aviation for 1928.

But this was only the beginning for Doc Oaks. While his Western Canada Airways continued to haul freight and do general bush flying, Oaks helped launch a more specialized outfit, Northern Aerial Minerals Exploration Ltd., or N.A.M.E., to fly prospectors into remote areas ahead of their rivals. Soon his planes were dipping into the mirrored surfaces of isolated lakes, letting prospectors or mining engineers scramble ashore to poke at mounds of rottenstone. Gray green in color and quick to crumble beneath a pick, it is the oldest rock found on the face of the earth, dating back more than 500 million years to the Pre-Cambrian era and containing gold, silver, platinum, nickel, zinc and copper.

Oaks and his fellow N.A.M.E. pilots soon found themselves criss-crossing Canada's mineral-rich but desolate Barrens from the Rockies to Hudson Bay, opening previously unexplored and unmapped territory. Oaks set up fuel caches at strategic locations all over northern Canada, thereby increasing the range and safety of his flights. To make winter operations less painful, he and Cheesman developed the use of "nose hangars," small tents that fitted over the engine. Warmed by a small stove and protected from the worst windy blasts, a pilot or mechanic could work inside the nose hangar on his plane's engine without risking the agony of frostbitten fingers.

As N.A.M.E. prospered, Oaks bought some new Fairchild FC-1s. They were built by a firm that got into aircraft manufacture almost by accident. It nevertheless produced some of the finest small all-purpose planes ever seen, ones that seemed made to order for bush flying.

Sherman Fairchild, founder of the company, was a brilliant engineer who, toward the end of World War I, had devised the finest aerial reconnaissance camera yet seen. When the War ended and interest in his cameras evaporated, Fairchild decided to use them himself, founding Fairchild Aerial Surveys. His aerial mapping company was soon surveying large tracts of Canada, initially using rented aircraft. One particularly bitter winter's day, Fairchild was shocked to observe the degree to which his hired pilots and crew suffered from exposure in the open-cockpit aircraft they were using.

Back in the warmth of his hotel, Fairchild interviewed several of the pilots, eliciting descriptions of the sort of plane they fervently wished they had. It would be a high-winged monoplane to afford good downward visibility and, above all, it would have an enclosed, heated cabin. It would also be powered by an air-cooled radial engine to eliminate the problems caused at low temperatures by the liquid-cooled motors installed in many of the war-surplus aircraft still in use.

Fairchild founded an aircraft-manufacturing company in Farmingdale, Long Island, and swiftly produced his first three models, the FC-1, FC-1A and FC-2—F for Fairchild and C for that all-important closed cabin. Construction was kept simple—metal tubing with fabric covering—for easy repairs and overhaul, and the plane's designers, aeronautical engineers Norman McQueen and Alexander Klemin, added an innovative feature: hinges at the base of the wings so that they could be folded back for storage. The first Fairchilds were powered by 200-horsepower Wright Whirlwind radial engines, but later models such as the FC-2W, FC-51 and FC-71 usually had other radials, the extraordinarily reliable and more powerful 420-horsepower Pratt & Whitney Wasp or the 300-horsepower Wasp Junior.

The introduction of the first Fairchilds in 1927 ushered in the great age of bush flying in Canada. They could be outfitted with wheels, floats or skis, thus allowing pilots to fly year-round, an impossibility in the old HS-2L flying boats. The Fairchilds were smaller, easier to fly and marginally faster—not to say warmer—than the Fokkers, which had open cockpits for the pilot forward of their cabins. Yet the Fairchilds carried an

Coping with winter's cold

Winter in the far north—where boiling water tossed into the air would instantly freeze—elevated the simple chore of starting a plane's engine from a routine to a ritual. Even before a pilot landed he took special measures to ensure he could take off again, tapping the throttle during his approach to keep the engine from cooling. On the ground the pilot drained the oil tank and rushed the oil indoors before it had time to freeze.

To bring his aircraft back to life, a flier had to preheat the engine oil on a stove and warm the engine inside a nose hangar—often nothing more elaborate than a canvas shroud draped over the cowling. Heat for the engines came from a gasoline burner, called a blowpot, positioned just below the engine. The pilot then poured the hot oil into the tank, and with a little luck, the engine would start.

Because arousing an airplane from its frigid slumber could consume up to two hours, it was usually done in the darkness before sunrise; this allowed the pilot to cram as many flying hours as possible into the abbreviated arctic day. By first light the engine was warmed up and idling, and the aircraft stood ready once more to take off.

A pilot in eastern Manitoba stirs engine oil over a blowpot while the engine itself is warmed inside a nose hangar.

A bush plane is refueled from a primitive tanker while the engine warms. To keep the engine from cooling during flight some aviators rigged metal shields around the cylinders to protect them from the ravages of the icy wind.

A pilot in Sleetmute, Alaska, keeps the tarpaulin hung over the nose of his Fairchild Pilgrim from flapping into the open flame inside that is heating the engine. The plane's skis have been propped clear of the ice to prevent them from freezing in place.

A pair of Fokker Universals confront each other as they undergo maintenance while shielded by a glorified double nose hangar.

After landing on a northern lake, a tail-shrouded plane thaws out with the help of a stove whose pipe protrudes from the canvas.

equal payload. In short, although rather boxy and unlovely in appearance, they proved ideal planes for bush flying and were much copied by other manufacturers such as Stinson and Waco. Many Fairchilds remained in service from the 1920s until World War II, and even after.

Canadians such as Stuart Graham and Doc Oaks can be called the first true bush pilots, but their neighbors to the west, the Alaskans, were not far behind, taking up bush flying with enthusiasm in the mid-1920s. In Alaska, however, the emphasis was different. In Canada, exploration and development provided the principal motivation, and simply getting around more easily in the backwoods was secondary. In Alaska it was the reverse; prospecting and exploring by plane were important, but just getting around was so difficult that bush planes quickly became a vital part of everyday life, changing the personality and spurring the growth of the immense territory.

Alaska's first bush pilot was Carl Ben Eielson, a North Dakota farm boy of Scandinavian descent who learned to fly during World War I. Like many other veterans of the American Air Service, he barnstormed for a couple of years, but when he arrived in Alaska in 1922 it was as a teacher, newly hired to give math and science courses at the Fairbanks high school. The flying bug proved too powerful. Eielson soon persuaded several citizens to help him acquire a Curtiss JN-4, the famous Jenny trainer of the War. When it arrived, crated, from the States, he assembled it in a corner of the town's baseball park, Weeks Field.

Once he had put the Jenny in flying condition, Eielson was besieged by the people of Fairbanks, who flocked to Weeks Field demanding to be taken up for their first airplane rides. He began ferrying people and goods to nearby settlements, becoming the first pilot to carry passengers in central Alaska. Then, attempting to put his small air service on a businesslike basis, Eielson got in touch with the postal authorities in Washington, asking for a contract to fly the mail. The Post Office obliged, and in 1924 Eielson, having acquired a de Havilland 4, made eight mail runs in the plane from Fairbanks to the town of McGrath, 280 miles away. But three crash landings left the postal officials sour on the project and they withdrew their financial support. Eielson folded up his flying service and for a time left Alaska.

During Eielson's absence, a number of other adventurous pilots arrived, seeing in the vast and largely unsettled territory the ideal place to start bush air services. First among them was Noel Wien, another large, even-tempered farm boy of Scandinavian ancestry, who had grown up in rural Minnesota. Wien started in Anchorage, assembling a war-surplus open-cockpit biplane called a Standard J-1 with a 150-horsepower Hispano-Suiza engine. He soon moved his fledgling operation from coastal Anchorage to inland Fairbanks. His flight to Fairbanks on July 6, 1924, was a foretaste of the sort of perils he would face again and again in those earliest days of Alaskan flying, involving as it did flying over the Alaska Range, of which Mount

After arriving by ship from the United States, a wingless Fokker Super Universal belonging to Northern Air Transport, Inc., a Fairbanks bush-flying outfit, is loaded onto a railway flatcar at the southern Alaska port of Cordova. At a frozen lake a few miles up the track—the nearest place for a takeoff—the plane was unloaded and its wings were attached. Then pilot Hans Mirow flew it the remaining 325 miles or so inland to Fairbanks.

McKinley, the tallest mountain in North America, is the key feature.

To take full advantage of Alaska's long summer hours of daylight and the stable early-morning air, he took off at 2:30 a.m. with his mechanic, Bill Yunker, in the front cockpit. All Wien had to guide him over some very wild country was an Alaska Railroad company map, with inaccurate scale, that showed only the most significant curves and stations on the railroad's 356-mile Anchorage-Fairbanks route. Cruising along at a ground speed of 65 to 70 miles an hour at 2,000 feet, he followed the tracks to where they crossed the Knik and Matanuska Rivers, then took a shortcut, following another stream, the Susitna, keeping clear of a 4,000-foot peak on the left and 8,000-footers on the right.

Soon he faced the 20,320-foot majesty of Mount McKinley, flanked by huge glaciers. Flying to the east of McKinley's powerful snowy mass, Wien passed over the settlement of Talkeetna 80 miles north of Anchorage, and picking up the railway again, followed its tracks through the tortuous turns of Chulitna Pass. After navigating the pass, he climbed to 8,000 feet, clearing the lowest divide in the formidable Alaska Range.

The worst part of the flight, from Wien's point of view, still lay ahead. Nowhere in the rocky wilderness below was there any sign of a place where a forced landing would be possible, and he frequently lost sight of the tracks, since the railroad went through three long tunnels. Then suddenly real trouble loomed. Dead ahead Wien saw a thick pall of smoke, evidently the result of a huge brush fire, obscuring the tracks and masking the outline of some more hills. With no place to land, he had

Canada's eagles of the Arctic

In the 1920s and 1930s, Canada's inhospitable far north posed severe challenges to bush pilots. They lacked not only two-way radios, but proper maps to show them the way. Often their only guide was a grizzled prospector attempting to pick out from the air landmarks he knew on the ground. Moreover, they could not always trust their compasses, because mineral deposits could set the needle to drifting crazily. And the closer they flew to the Magnetic North Pole, above the Arctic Circle, the less reliable the compasses became.

Yet in spite of such limitations, the best of these pilots managed the near impossible, completing flights of many hundreds of miles across the wilderness. In the process, they helped to open the north's treasure chest of minerals and to establish regular passenger and mail routes.

Pilot Grant McConachie inaugurated regular airmail service to the Yukon Territory. In the fall of 1932, he rescued two gas explosion victims from a wilderness camp, returning home with a split propeller held together by thin metal binding.

Legendary bush pioneer Punch Dickins, seen here (second from left) pausing for tea with his prospecting passengers, made a historic mapping flight across Canada's Barrens in 1928.

Tim Sims, seated second from left with sunbathing companions in 1935, served as an engineer on the 1,600-mile inaugural airmail flight from Alberta to Aklavik on the Arctic Ocean.

Widely heralded for his many successful search-and-rescue missions, Pat Reid (right) pioneered the first aerial route through Canada's Northwest Passage in 1929.

Herbert Hollick-Kenyon was a lead pilot on a 1929 search for members of the MacAlpine expedition, who were rescued after two months at Cambridge Bay above the Arctic Circle.

Wop May (right, with mechanic) made the first winter flight to the Arctic Ocean in 1929, piloting a Bellanca loaded with mail for isolated settlers.

Noel Wien points with chagrin to the ice-encrusted engine of his Stinson biplane after being downed by a windstorm en route from Nome to Elephant Point in 1928. Forced to wait out the gale at Candle, Alaska, Wien and his passengers finally completed the flight a week later than planned.

little choice but to plunge into the smoke. To keep the rails in sight, he dropped to a mere 100 feet and manipulated the controls so that the plane flew twisted on its side. That way he could at least see straight down. "Pretty soon I was too busy even to worry," Wien recalled. "I kept my eyes down on those rails and my hands and feet loose but ready on the controls, making every turn. My eyes began to sting a little from smoke getting into my goggles."

Suddenly Yunker waved his arms and pointed down. To the left of the rails they could dimly make out a big cleared area—the experimental farm belonging to the new college in Fairbanks. Completing the historic first flight ever made over the Alaska Range, Wien and Yunker, nearly blind, groped their way to a landing at tiny Weeks Field. There they found a handful of people waiting for them. Bill Yunker jumped down and angrily demanded why the members of the greeting committee had not telegraphed word of the smoke to Anchorage so that he and Wien could have postponed the flight. "We've been in this stuff for 80 miles," he howled. "You want to lose your plane and pilot without ever laying eyes on them?" It turned out that the smoke had been cloaking the area for two weeks and everybody thought Wien had heard about it. "Yunker was really peeved," said the imperturbable pilot, "but I figured we'd made it, so no use yelling about it."

Flying out of Fairbanks, Wien soon became Alaska's most respected

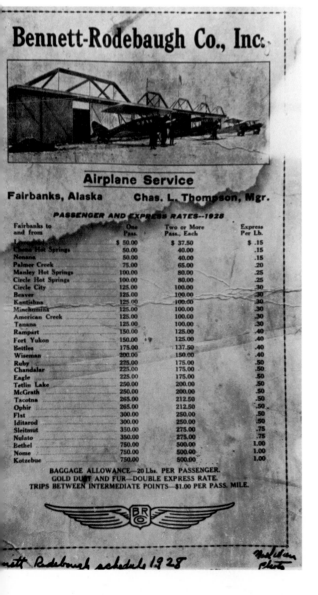

A list of fares and destinations published by the Bennett-Rodebaugh Co. in 1928 shows that even the most remote Alaskan settlements had become accessible by air. In 1929, Bennett-Rodebaugh, along with other transport companies, was bought out by the Aviation Corporation of America to form Alaskan Airways.

Bennett-Rodebaugh Co., Inc.

Airplane Service

Fairbanks, Alaska   **Chas. L. Thompson, Mgr.**

PASSENGER AND EXPRESS RATES--1928

Fairbanks to and from	One Pass.	Two or More Pass., Each	Express Per Lb.
	$ 50.00	$ 37.50	$ .15
Chena Hot Springs	50.00	40.00	.15
Nenana	50.00	40.00	.15
Palmer Creek	75.00	65.00	.20
Manley Hot Springs	100.00	80.00	.25
Circle Hot Springs	100.00	80.00	.25
Circle City	125.00	100.00	.30
Beaver	125.00	100.00	.30
Kantishna	125.00	100.00	.30
Minchumina	125.00	100.00	.30
American Creek	125.00	100.00	.30
Tanana	125.00	100.00	.30
Rampart	150.00	125.00	.40
Fort Yukon	150.00	125.00	.40
Bettles	175.00	137.50	.40
Wiseman	200.00	150.00	.40
Ruby	225.00	175.00	.50
Chandalar	225.00	175.00	.50
Eagle	225.00	175.00	.50
Tetlin Lake	250.00	200.00	.50
McGrath	250.00	200.00	.50
Tacotna	265.00	212.50	.50
Ophir	265.00	212.50	.50
Flat	300.00	250.00	.50
Iditarod	300.00	250.00	.50
Sleitmut	350.00	275.00	.75
Nulato	350.00	275.00	.75
Bethel	750.00	500.00	1.00
Nome	750.00	500.00	1.00
Kotzebue	750.00	500.00	1.00

BAGGAGE ALLOWANCE—20 Lbs. PER PASSENGER.
GOLD DUST AND FUR—DOUBLE EXPRESS RATE.
TRIPS BETWEEN INTERMEDIATE POINTS—$1.00 PER PASS. MILE.

bush pilot, building up an admirable safety record and a remarkable list of firsts, including being the first aviator in either Alaska or Canada to fly north of the Arctic Circle and the first to fly from North America to the Soviet Union, crossing the Bering Strait from Nome to Siberia's North Cape. A self-contained man given to massive silences, Noel Wien possessed two qualities essential to the survival of a pilot in Alaska: tenacity and painstaking caution. If the weather looked uncertain, he would stubbornly refuse to fly no matter how much his passengers pleaded with him that the trip was urgent. Once he did take off, he would not let his mind wander. "I never flew relaxed or daydreamed," he once said, "but was continually looking for possible landing spots. Where would I land if the motor conked out? I was looking, looking, looking."

When Wien began flying, there was no such thing as an emergency landing field anywhere in Alaska, and few of the widely scattered towns and villages had yet stirred themselves—airplanes being so new in the territory—to hack airstrips from the surrounding forest or bush. Good paved airfields simply did not exist. Wien found himself navigating with inadequate maps over trackless mountain fastnesses or endless stretches of muskeg that became featureless frozen plains in winter. Having no radio, he could not signal his position should he be forced down—supposing he knew where he was—and any rescue parties sent to find a lost plane would have had to travel, probably for weeks, by dog sled. His only navigational aid at first was a small compass, and even this was of dubious value, since he often flew so near the Magnetic Pole that the needle gave him false directions.

To find his way Wien was forced to memorize thousands of subtle landmarks such as rock outcroppings and oddly shaped lakes. The best places to land in emergencies, he found, were the sand bars or stretches of hard-packed gravel common in Alaska's many rivers. He became so adept at bringing his old Standard down on these bars, stalling the plane in softly, that he routinely used them as landing fields when taking people or freight into the many isolated settlements he served.

Wien soon learned that even extreme caution was not always enough when flying between the small settlements in Alaska's huge interior. On a trip in May of 1925 to the gold-mining outpost of Wiseman, north of the Arctic Circle, Wien made one of his usual sand-bar landings in the middle of the Koyukuk River. After a tumultuous welcome from Wiseman's citizens—no plane had ever been there before—he refueled and took off again, heading back toward Fairbanks. But strong head winds slowed his progress to less than 40 miles an hour and after three hours Wien still had not spotted his halfway landmark, the Yukon River. Finally the Yukon appeared below and he made a stop near the settlement of Rampart, landing on the river, which was still iced over.

Buying some fuel, he resumed his flight. But as soon as he had gained altitude he found the head winds had become even worse. Airplanes are capable of flying into 60-mile-an-hour winds, he recalled thinking at the time, "but they can't get anywhere." Wien turned southward, plan-

Dressed in a caribou parka stitched by Eskimo women, pilot Ben Eielson arrives in Point Barrow, Alaska, in 1929. The previous year, he and explorer Hubert Wilkins became the first men to cross the Arctic Ocean by plane when they flew a single-engined Lockheed Vega from Point Barrow to Spitsbergen in Norway.

ning an emergency landing at Nenana, the nearest settlement, but the gale kept pushing him off course. Soon his fuel-gauge needle again pointed toward empty and the oil pressure in the engine had dipped dangerously low. He picked out a snow-covered sand bar on the Toklat River and swooped toward it. Just as the undercarriage touched down, a piece of driftwood hidden under the snow snatched at the right wheel. The plane stopped dead, the right wing dug into the snow and the landing gear shattered. Wien was utterly alone, at 10:45 at night with the subarctic twilight deepening, with no radio and with the temperature just above freezing. He figured he was at least 40 miles from Nenana.

Wien ate one of the whole-wheat rolls he had bought that morning at a Fairbanks bakery and then dozed through the brief night in the cockpit. Awakening when it became light at 2:30, he ate his last roll and began walking. He knew the direction he should take, since he could see in the distance two unmistakable landmarks, the Alaska Range and the huge eminence of Mount McKinley. Wading through a shallow spot in the Toklat, he struck out across the already thawing muskeg. "I'd take two or three steps through the soggy snow and mud," he later recalled, "and one leg would go down to the hip. I'd pull it out and take a few more steps and, again, down to the hip."

After an hour of this agonizing effort, Wien fell forward and remained motionless, panting. "I couldn't have wiggled a toe even if a grizzly was heading for me," he later said. But eventually he got up and struggled on, resting again every so often. After 18 hours of struggle he had covered 10 miles. Sleeping again briefly despite attacks by swarms of the ferocious mosquitoes that come out early in the Alaskan spring, he gained enough strength to slog on through a second day. He crossed one river by using the small ax he carried to chop down a tree so that the trunk fell across to the far bank, and he later made his way across another on a small raft he lashed together. He found some wild cranberries and ate them, which gave him the strength to keep going through another day, when he finally reached the village of Nenana.

Wien had lost 20 pounds and was suffering from a bad cold, but he was otherwise undamaged. He received a hero's welcome in Fairbanks when he arrived there from Nenana on a "gas speeder," a motorized railroad handcar. Interviewed by a reporter on his return, Wien allowed, in an apotheosis of understatement, that the experience had been "uncomfortable." It made him even more cautious than before; he never flew again without a full survival kit that included several weeks' supply of concentrated foods, a couple of guns and an array of tools. Between this gear and the baggage brought along by the passengers, Wien's Standard—which he rescued from its sand bar—often took on the aspect of a rural Mexican bus. Fresh groceries, canned goods, picks and shovels were stowed in every available cranny, while bedrolls and suitcases sprouted from the passenger cockpit along with the fur-capped heads of his clients. For all but summer flying Wien himself coped with the sub-zero temperatures by wearing an outlandish coat made of Australian wombat fur with a wolfskin collar over several layers of wool.

In 1926 Noel Wien quit the Fairbanks charter business when his nonflying partner hired a pilot whom Wien thought careless. Noel's brother Ralph, an expert mechanic who had moved to Alaska to service the Standard and a newly acquired Fokker F.III, left with him. By 1927, however, the Wiens were back in operation with a new partner named Gene Miller, founding a bush-flying service in Nome, an isolated settlement on the Bering Sea, 560 miles west of Fairbanks. Here Noel, at first using the same battered Standard, opened up routes to several more communities, many north of the Arctic Circle, that had never before seen a plane. Especially astonished were the Eskimos, who dubbed the Standard a "moose ptarmigan"—a huge, moose-sized bird.

The new business, named Wien Alaska Airways, prospered sufficiently for Miller and the Wiens to acquire another aircraft, a handsomely equipped Stinson cabin biplane. It had a Wright Whirlwind radial engine, more instruments than Wien had ever seen before, brakes (another new luxury) and a phenomenal range of 800 miles with an extra built-in fuel tank. Best of all, the pilot sat inside the cabin, out of the wind. With the Stinson the Wien brothers inaugurated the first regular service between Nome and Fairbanks—a route that crossed no fewer than three mountain systems—flew medical mercy missions throughout Alaska's far north and instituted service to remote Point Barrow on the Arctic Ocean. They also ran the first winter air service ever seen in interior Alaska. "For the first time in the history of Nome," Noel Wien later wrote, "the last boat leaving in October didn't mean isolation from the States until the first boat in the next June."

In 1928 the Wiens added another aircraft, an all-metal Hamilton monoplane that cost the then astronomical sum of $26,000. A 420-horsepower Wasp engine gave the Hamilton a cruising speed 50 miles an hour faster than the old Standard's; it carried six passengers in its heated cabin or 2,300 pounds of freight. This plane, NC 10002, was destined to become famous—for its successes and for its tragic end.

In February 1929, Wien received an unusual offer. A fur-trading schooner, the *Elisif,* was icebound off North Cape, a forbidding part of Siberia on the Arctic Ocean largely unknown even to the Russians, with a load of valuable furs in her hold. Her owner, Olaf Swenson, wanted Wien to fly the furs out to market. Nobody had yet flown from Asia to America or from America to Asia across the Bering Strait, and the Soviet government resisted such contact. But Swenson's furs originated in the Soviet Union and his relations with Moscow were amicable. So flights to Siberia this time would be permissible.

On March 7, Wien, accompanied by mechanic Calvin "Doc" Cripe, took off from Nome in the new Hamilton to find the *Elisif.* It took only 17 minutes to cross the Bering Strait from Alaska's Seward Peninsula to the Asian shore, and the weather was so clear and still that Wien figured the flight to North Cape should take only another four hours. The flight was not, however, to be trouble-free. Once the plane was over Siberia, the oil pressure in its Wasp engine began to rise alarmingly. Wien realized that frost must have formed in the oil-tank vent tube, which was located on the leading edge of the right wing. They would soon be in trouble unless Cripe could do something about it. Opening the right cockpit window, Cripe reached out and, by stretching as far as he could, just managed to scrape out the frost with the tip of a long knife—a process he repeated every few minutes despite the 40-below temperature outside for the rest of the trip. At last they sighted the cape and near it a black speck that grew into a three-masted schooner. Wien came down on the pack ice for one of the roughest landings of his career, bouncing the two men out of their seats: The shock absorbers had frozen.

The next day, *Elisif* crewmen loaded the Hamilton with heavy bales of fox pelts, and Wien just managed to get aloft. The return trip was far from easy. He had been obliged to take on 70 gallons of Soviet fuel from a cache that was 10 years old. It proved to be inferior in quality; all the way back to Alaska the Wasp ran rough. Again Cripe was forced to

A desperate search at the edge of the world

The disappearance of famed aviator Ben Eielson and his mechanic, Earl Borland, off the Siberian coast in November 1929 touched off one of the longest and most frustrating rescue efforts in the history of arctic flying. The pair vanished while attempting to pick up furs from an icebound schooner named the *Nanuk*. But gale-force winds and 40° below zero temperatures grounded the half-dozen or so U.S., Canadian and Soviet planes that assembled to search the area.

It was not until mid-December that two planes, piloted through a blinding snowstorm by Americans Joe Crosson and Harold Gillam, made it out to the *Nanuk* to set up a rescue base. The weather remained so vile that Crosson and Gillam managed only eight flying days in the next five weeks. The two fliers spent those days combing an area 60 miles east of the *Nanuk* where Siberians had spotted a plane overhead in November. But the searchers found nothing.

The two aircraft soon exhausted the gasoline on board the ship and were returning to Alaska for more when Crosson spotted a dark streak on the snow. The fliers realized it was the shadow of a wing and on landing found the crushed cabin of Eielson's plane. But there was no trace of its occupants. The next day, a break in the weather enabled some of the other search planes to reach the *Nanuk* and begin hauling men and supplies to the crash site.

For 22 days, rescuers dug through the snow around the wreck. On February 16, more than three months after the aviators had vanished, Borland's frozen body was uncovered; two days later Eielson's was found 120 feet from the plane. Both men, hurled from their seats by the impact of the crash, had died instantly.

ARCTIC OCEAN

★• North Cape

SIBERIA

ALASKA

Anchorage

• Teller

• Nome

BERING SEA

A star marks the crash site in the frozen Arctic Ocean.

Two of the planes assembled for the search for Ben Eielson stand on the ice beside the trading vessel Nanuk.

Soviet, Canadian and U.S. planes parked on the ice near the Nanuk await a break in the weather. Joe Crosson's Waco biplane is at far right.

In a picture taken by Harold Gillam, Crosson stands beneath the wing of Eielson's wrecked plane just after the pair spotted it from the air.

Teams of rescue workers begin the grim task of digging through the hard-packed snow to find the bodies of the downed aviators.

The bodies of Eielson and Borland, draped in American flags stitched out of red, white and blue muslin by Siberian Eskimo women, are turned over to the Americans by Soviet officials at a brief ceremony near the Nanuk on March 4, 1930.

Weary members of the international search team prepare to load the aviators' bodies aboard a Fairchild for the flight from Siberia back to Alaska.

repeatedly chip frost from the oil-tank vent. It was with great relief that the two men lumbered into Nome. They had succeeded, however, in making one of the most difficult bush-flying trips ever attempted.

Noel Wien's success encouraged a similar attempt the following autumn, when another of Olaf Swenson's schooners, the *Nanuk,* became stuck in the ice at North Cape. This time the fur trader offered $50,000 to any bush pilot willing to fly from Alaska to airlift out the furs. Noel Wien, in the United States on a honeymoon with his new wife, Ada, was unavailable. But by 1929 Ben Eielson had returned to Alaska, had started an air service and had purchased the all-metal Hamilton from the Wiens. To Eielson, Swenson's offer of $50,000 seemed like just the sort of deal he needed to put his new air service on its feet. He accepted.

Eielson himself led the expedition, flying the Hamilton with mechanic Earl Borland. They were accompanied by another bush pilot, Frank Dorbandt, flying a Stinson cabin biplane. The two pilots set out on October 26 from Fairbanks, following roughly the same route used the previous February by Noel Wien, and reached the *Nanuk* at North Cape without incident. The Hamilton and the Stinson then flew out loaded with furs, taking six crew members as well.

Eielson and Dorbandt planned a second trip, but fierce weather pinned them down at Teller, their jumping-off place on Alaska's Seward Peninsula 80 miles north of Nome. Finally, on the gloomy morning of November 9, the able but impulsive Dorbandt, chafing at the delay, got in the Stinson and roared away. Eielson, against his better judgment, followed in the Hamilton.

Dorbandt, finding blizzards alternating with heavy fog over the Bering Strait, turned back and landed at Teller. Eielson and mechanic Borland simply vanished, swallowed up in the fog and snow.

The disappearance of Eielson and Borland produced headlines around the world. Aviators from Alaska joined with Soviet fliers in searching for the missing plane, and Canadian pilots from the Ontario Provincial Air Service and Doc Oaks's N.A.M.E. also took part.

Despite valiant efforts by the Canadian contingent, led by N.A.M.E.'s Pat Reid, it was a pair of Eielson's friends, Alaskan bush pilots Joe Crosson and Harold Gillam, who reached the *Nanuk* first, having risked everything to fly to North Cape in a pair of small open-cockpit aircraft. Taking off on search patrols in their two planes from the ice next to the ship, the two Alaskan aviators scanned the ice and snow along the Siberian coast and eventually located the downed aircraft *(page 43)*. There was no sign of either Eielson or Borland, dead or alive, and it was too risky to land for a closer look. Finally, three months after the disappearance, a party of Siberian Chukchi who had been enlisted in the search discovered the bodies of the two men buried in snow. Evidently the aviators had plunged into that most dreaded of arctic phenomena, a total whiteout—snow below and only white drifting fog all about. In such a situation a pilot had little way to tell whether he was in a climb or a dive, a slip or a stall. It seemed clear from the evidence of the crash that

Eielson, unable to judge the Hamilton's flying angle and betrayed by a faulty altimeter, had smashed into the ice pack at full speed.

That Harold Gillam was one of the two pilots to find Eielson's plane was, Alaskans later decided, no surprise. At the time of the search, Gillam had yet to earn a pilot's license and had only 40 hours at the controls. Yet he beat the veteran Joe Crosson to the *Nanuk,* barreling straight through fog at full throttle, regardless of danger. As silent and self-contained as Noel Wien, Gillam was in other regards Wien's exact opposite—probably the least careful bush pilot in Alaskan history.

In 1931 Gillam pioneered bush flying in the copper-mining district inland from Cordova on Alaska's southern coast, east of Anchorage. It was perhaps the most difficult place in Alaska to fly—a mountainous region often blanketed by sea-bred storms, fogs and turbulent air. The mine airstrip he frequently used was a narrow clearing hacked into the top of a small plateau. "If you undershot," another flier said, "you ran into a bluff—and when you took off, you hadn't a foot to spare." Under such conditions, it was little wonder that in his first six months of operation, Gillam had six crack-ups. No serious injuries resulted, but Gillam was soon $30,000 in debt to his backers for planes and repairs.

What made Gillam a legend in Alaska was his uncanny ability—and his willingness—to fly through weather so foul that it grounded every other aviator in the territory. A pilot named Oscar Winchell who worked with Gillam for a time recalled taking a trip with his boss through "Gillam weather." The clouds and fog were so thick that the two fliers were forced up to 16,000 feet to ride over them. Gillam seemed unworried as the fuel gauge dropped toward zero and still no breaks showed in the clouds below. Although they were over mountains, Gillam finally throttled back and unconcernedly took the plane down, descending in great circles through the blinding, swirling fog. When they finally broke out into the clear the plane was right over the airfield. Gillam landed, Winchell recalled, and then got out, refusing to taxi toward the hangar. What the wordless Gillam did not bother to explain to Winchell was that he could not taxi—the fuel tank was bone-dry.

Gillam was not alone in setting himself difficult flying tasks. One of his contemporaries, Bob Reeve, became a legend for his uncanny skill at landing on Alaska's glaciers, a feat no other pilot had even attempted. Reeve had begun his career in Latin America, flying mail over the Andes, but had spent the money he made so swiftly that he went broke. Heading north to Alaska to start life over, he arrived in Anchorage in 1932 aboard a coastal steamer as a stowaway. Virtually his only possessions were a pair of worn aviator's boots and a ragged leather coat.

He soon learned, however, that a crippled Eaglerock, a small open-cockpit machine, was sitting in a hangar at Valdez down the coast, waiting for repair. So Reeve stowed away again for Valdez. There he showed the Eaglerock's owner his logbooks, which proved he had 3,000 hours in the air, and offered to lease the plane once it was

The ready wit and humor of Bob Reeve, one of Alaska's boldest bush pilots, is revealed by signs adorning his car and headquarters. The one on the side wall of the shack reads: "Unlicensed and nuts? Always use Reeve Airways. Slow-Unreliable Unfair And Crooked. Scared & Unlicensed. Reeve Airways 'The Best.'"

repaired. Meanwhile, he would be happy to put the plane in flying trim for a mere dollar an hour.

The deal was struck, Reeve repaired the plane—and then gave an exhibition of the sort of flying that would make him famous. Taking off in the Eaglerock, he headed right for the forbidding crags of the Chugach Mountains that overlook Valdez. Local pilots usually gave them a wide berth, but Reeve was a veteran of mountain flying and, besides, he knew nothing of local custom. He flew around the Chugach for an hour or so, astonishing the citizens of Valdez, including some local prospectors who had been searching for a way to penetrate the valleys of the towering range. Most of the accessible gold fields in Alaska had been worked out, they told Reeve, but there was still plenty of gold left deep in the interior, in rugged reaches like the Chugach, where it was virtually impossible for a prospector to trek overland with the necessary supplies. If Reeve could somehow fly them in, they could all become rich.

Reeve pondered the proposition. On his maiden flight he had encountered his first williwaws, sudden gusts of violent wind created by turbulence where glacier and mountain meet, and had had a good look at the mountains' saw-toothed peaks. He would also be forced to land on glaciers—ice fields covered in winter by fluffy new snow that hid deep fissures—or on old, rotten ice that was ready to give way and drop the pilot and his plane into 1,000-foot-deep chasms.

Despite his misgivings, Reeve agreed to take the sourdoughs into the Chugach. Having depleted his cash to buy a ski-equipped Fairchild FC-51, he was in desperate need of funds to pay for his groceries and fuel. The Chugach range, where nobody else would fly, became his unique niche in the world of bush pilots.

In the spring of 1933, Reeve flew a prospector deep into the mountain fastness for a preliminary look at Brevier Glacier. It was intimidating. The only possible spot to land was on a steep snow shelf barely 100 feet wide and 500 feet long. Nor was that the only problem: "There was no horizon to judge by, no perspective," Reeve recalled. "It all looked flat white. There was no way of telling how close you were to the snow."

Attempting a trial touchdown, Reeve miscalculated, stalled and crashed into a giant snowdrift. Nobody was hurt and nothing was wrong with the plane, but it took him and his passenger all afternoon to dig out. Once they had turned the plane around and had packed down the slope with their snowshoes, taking off downhill proved quick and easy. Inadvertently, Reeve had made his first glacier landing and takeoff, and it was now up to him to do it again the right way. "I didn't like the looks of it," he said, "but I had committed myself. Besides, I'd found that if you turn back that first time, it's liable to become a habit."

To provide perspective in the blinding whiteness of the snowy landscape, Reeve threw black-dyed gunny sacks down to serve as markers on the glacier. He was then able to make his approach on a steep climb at full power, judge his position and the slope of the glacier from the markers, touch his skis down—and cut the throttle. The steep grade

Mountain climber Bradford Washburn (left) stands ankle-deep in mud on the Valdez flats with pilot Bob Reeve in 1937, just before Reeve flew Washburn and a climbing party to Mount Lucania in the Canadian Yukon. Reeve had removed the plane's cabin door to quickly jettison extra baggage in an emergency.

Reeve's high-winged Fairchild FC-51 kicks up a spray of muddy water during a 1937 takeoff from the Valdez mud flats. By using the flats as a runway in summer, Reeve could continue to employ skis, which he needed to ferry mountaineers or prospectors into Alaska's glaciers, snow-clad throughout the entire year.

slowed the Fairchild nicely, allowing him to stop within the 500 feet available. At the upper end of the slope, Reeve turned his plane sideways to keep it from sliding back down on its skis. Once he had the system worked out, his landings were trouble-free. He also discovered how to land and take off at Valdez on skis in summer. He simply availed himself of the port city's tidal mud flats: When the tide was out, it left a surface ooze that was like chocolate pudding—well suited to the skis. He went on in the following year to take dozens of prospectors and many tons of mining equipment into the Chugach, using as a landing zone what came to be called Reeve Glacier.

News of Reeve's extraordinary mud flat-to-glacier flights reached faraway Boston and the ears of Bradford Washburn, a Harvard instructor, mountaineer and explorer who later became director of the Boston Museum of Science and the world's leading expert on the mountains of Alaska. In 1937, when most of those mountains were virtually unknown, Washburn planned one of his first trips to Alaska to explore and map them. Writing Reeve beforehand, he asked whether the pilot could take a climbing party to Mount Lucania, a 17,150-foot peak in the isolated southwest corner of the Canadian Yukon, landing on nearby Walsh Glacier at 8,500 feet. Reeve clinched the deal with a terse telegram: ANYWHERE YOU'LL RIDE I'LL FLY.

Reeve succeeded easily in taking in two members of Washburn's four-man team and most of its gear. But the last inbound flight, carrying Washburn and team member Robert Bates, proved perilous. An approaching storm made the air rough as they came in over the glacier.

Below them was a grotesque wasteland of sheer cliffs, deep crevasses and boulders. Reeve at last spotted the cache of gear he had deposited on his previous trips. Swiftly, he made his approach through a low overcast and landed. The snow was softening rapidly in the warm air. The plane might plunge through the snow cover and slide into a crevasse at any moment. Hurriedly, the three men struggled to position the Fairchild on a firmer base.

Reeve could not risk a takeoff, however, until a slight cold snap came and with it a light snowfall. Days passed. Repeatedly the men tried to prepare the plane for takeoff, only to have it sink into the slush. But after four nights the temperature fell and new snow put a fresh cover on the glacier. In the morning Reeve prepared to take the gamble. He knew he would have only one shot. If it failed, he was as good as dead.

Reeve barreled down the glacier, plunged through the crust into a deep hole, roared out the other side and kept going. It looked as if he would never lift off. Then he saw a smooth, sloping sheet of ice to one side. He veered in that direction and roared over the icefall into space. At first the plane plummeted straight down, but then the Fairchild reached flying speed and swooped up just shy of the glacier's bottom.

Watching from above, Washburn saw the Fairchild reappear like a phoenix rising from a pit and go flying off. "Bates and I were simply spellbound," Washburn said. "It was a desperate maneuver which for almost any other pilot would have been suicidal. We shrieked for joy."

The news of this feat was widely reported in newspapers, but Reeve's fame did him little good financially. Despite living from hand to mouth, he somehow purchased a second Fairchild, but by the end of 1939 he had lost both planes. The first suffered severe engine trouble; the second and better aircraft was picked up by a howling windstorm and badly damaged. Reeve was rescued from penury by Noel Wien. As kind a man as he was an exceptional pilot, Wien gave Reeve a job hauling cargo, which tided the glacier pilot through the worst of his hard times. Then came World War II, and flying in Alaska was forever changed.

Even before the War, the growth of aviation in the territory had been remarkable. In 1924 Noel Wien and his old Standard had been virtually alone, but a dozen years later, in 1936, seventy-five aircraft served Alaska's widely scattered settlements. On the eve of the conflict in 1939 there were 175 planes and, remarkably, more than 100 landing fields.

The War brought paved airfields, weather reports and electronic navigational aids unimagined by the early bush pilots, and Wien prospered to a degree he had never dreamed of. Success forced him from the cockpit and into a swivel chair to help run his burgeoning company, renamed Wien Air Alaska in 1973. Five years earlier, he had acquired the first of five Boeing 737 jetliners. The jets were far outnumbered, however, by his fleet of smaller short-hop aircraft. With these, the company continued to serve Wien's beloved Alaska, making calls at no fewer than 190 airfields in the huge territory that, thanks in part to its bush pilots, had grown into the 49th state.

Atop Brevier Glacier, Reeve, his plane and a passenger are framed in splendid isolation 6,000 feet above sea level by peaks of the Chugach range.

The land of many waters

With water making up nearly 8 per cent of its landscape, Canada offered ready-made landing sites for pioneer bush pilots and their floatplanes in summer. Ontario alone boasted some 250,000 lakes. And when the lakes and rivers froze over in winter, their surfaces could be used by aircraft fitted with skis.

By the end of the 1920s there was scarcely a spot in Canada to which bush pilots were not prepared to go, or a region that lacked a bush-service operation. But the ability to fly the long distances between outposts depended upon one thing—refueling. To make this possible, 45-gallon drums were stored at regular intervals, most often at trading posts, but sometimes in the wilderness itself.

Mirrored in the Quebec lake that served as their headquarters, three floatplanes of Dominion Skyways await their pilots and cargoes in 1935.

Patrolling salmon fisheries off the coast of British Columbia, a Boeing flying boat operated by Western Canada Airways noses up to a trio of fishing vessels

gathered in an inlet. Government inspectors used the flying boat to detect trawlers that were fishing illegally in protected waters.

A D.H.60 Moth biplane and two Fairchild FC-2s hug the shore of the Harricana River at General Airways' base in the mining town of Amos, Quebec.

During a photographic survey of Canada's Yukon Territory in the summer of 1933, a Junkers W 34 at Carcross encounters a more traditional form of

transport—the stern-wheeler S.S. Tutski. Unlike the airplane, the paddle-wheeler could ply its route only in the North Country's short summer.

Near the Arctic Circle in the 1930s, a Western Canada Airways Fokker floatplane breaks the desolation of a lake deep in the Northwest Territories.

2

Adventurers of the Outback

The father of Australian aviation was, appropriately enough, the island continent's World War I Prime Minister, an irascible, brilliant, ruthless little man named William M. "Billy" Hughes. His way of stimulating flying in Australia was highly unorthodox. He proposed that there be an air race from England to Darwin, on Australia's northern coast—a route covering some 11,000 miles. And he proposed this in 1919, when even the best aircraft were fortunate to fly 500 miles nonstop, when air routes were unmapped and airfields were virtually unknown outside Europe and the United States. In short, Billy Hughes was asking the young aviators of the time to risk their necks trying to perform an almost impossible feat. Only the prize offered seemed sensible: £10,000 in a day when a pound was worth five dollars and five dollars was worth many times what it is today.

Hughes's wild scheme to publicize flying and bring it to Australia caused a storm of controversy in the country's press, as he knew it would. But he lashed his proposal through, fired by his conviction that Australia needed aviation to grow and prosper. Competition between the combatants of World War I to produce better and better warplanes had immeasurably speeded the development of aircraft. Hundreds of young Australians had learned to fly during the War after enlisting in Britain's Royal Flying Corps or Naval Air Service, or in Australia's own Flying Corps. Hughes himself knew better than most statesmen of the time what airplanes could do; while attending the Paris Peace Conference, he had commuted by air between a Paris airfield and hospitals in England, where he paid visits to Australian war wounded.

Hughes's perception of the benefits aviation could bestow on the country was realistic and farsighted. The enormous continent, almost exactly the same size as the United States at the time, was a transportation nightmare in 1919. The four principal cities to the east and south—Brisbane, Sydney, Melbourne and Adelaide—were widely separated on a coastline 1,500 miles long. A rail trip from Brisbane to Melbourne took at least three days. Smaller towns were dotted between the cities on a coastal fringe threaded by a majority of the nation's few roads and fewer rail lines. As for Perth on the western coast, it was connected with the cities on the east coast only by a single rail line; the 2,700-mile train trip from Perth to Brisbane took a week or more.

But the problems of getting from one city to another were insignificant compared with the difficulties of penetrating the interior—the great

Charles Kingsford-Smith displays the cockiness characteristic of pioneer bush pilots down under. In 1927, to demonstrate that Australia's coastal cities and towns could be connected by air, he and copilot Charles Ulm flew around the island continent's 7,500-mile perimeter in an unheard-of 10 days 5½ hours.

sun-baked wilderness the Australians call the Outback. In 1919, when Hughes proposed his air race, 90 per cent of Australia was accessible only on horseback or by oxcart or camel caravan. Travelers could go for days without seeing anyone else. Besides the isolation, there were the killing heat waves between May and September, the five parched months known as the "Dry," followed by flash floods that swept all before them in the soul-destroying "Wet" of winter's monsoons.

Yet this forbidding wilderness was essential to Australia's economy, for it was there that ranchers on spreads, or stations, as huge as any in Texas, bred the sheep whose wool fed the world's looms. Few of Australia's five million people in 1919 did not directly or indirectly rely on the wool business for their living. But apart from a few forlorn rail lines that straggled into the Outback to haul the wool to the ports, the far-flung sheep stations, and the little towns they occasionally spawned, had no direct links with the coastal cities or with one another.

A measure of the sheep graziers' isolation was their general inability to persuade women to marry them and live on the ranches. Women feared not only the boredom, but also getting pregnant. The nearest medical aid might be 10 days away by oxcart. A large percentage of Outback wives in the early years died in childbirth. For that matter, any medical emergency—appendicitis, an arm mangled in farm machinery—could prove deadly. Only with the coming of the airplane—and bush piloting—was this extreme and potentially fatal isolation relieved.

Billy Hughes's great air race did in fact make Australia air conscious, but the race itself was something of a fiasco. Although England was teeming with Australian combat pilots, only seven crews were able to raise the funds to purchase suitable aircraft. Of those seven, only two were to reach Australia. The remainder crashed along the way. Neither their hastily converted war-surplus planes nor their piloting expertise was equal to the task of flying halfway around the world.

Nevertheless, when a converted Vickers Vimy bomber bearing registration letters G-EAOU reached the port of Darwin in 27 days and 20 hours, all Australia celebrated. Suddenly the world had shrunk and Hughes's predictions of air links with Europe and services criss-crossing the continent seemed possible. Aircraft were no longer regarded as novel toys, suitable only for thrill seeking and joy riding (Australia had seen its first barnstormers in 1912), but rather as a revolutionary form of transportation that would change forever the quality of Australian life.

Australians were eager for a taste of the air age, and there were plenty of pilots willing to oblige them, war veterans at the controls of surplus aircraft. In those early days, piloting a plane almost anywhere in Australia could be considered bush flying, and these intrepid airmen needed all the resourcefulness and courage they had to survive the harsh conditions they encountered. The heat during the Dry could reach 130°, scorching a pilot's hands if he touched metal. Such heat also thinned the air, reducing a plane's normal lift and making takeoff from the Out-

One of the five aircraft that failed to complete the England-to-Australia air race of 1919, a Blackburn Kangaroo bomber sits tail up in a field on Crete where it crash-landed. The navigator on the ill-fated flight was Captain Hubert Wilkins, who later earned fame as a polar explorer.

back's crude airfields doubly risky. Summer winds also sent huge dust clouds roiling across the interior. The Wet, on the other hand, could simply inundate huge sections of the Outback, flooding landing fields.

Yet the tough Australian bush pilots conquered these conditions and even remained cheerful living in remote Outback hamlets that consisted of little more than shacks with corrugated iron roofs that either thundered during rains or broiled the occupants during the hot season. The pilots and their planes quickly became indispensable links between the Outback and civilization, carrying sheep shearers and prospectors, doctors and their medicines, necessary supplies and even luxuries into improvised airstrips hundreds of miles from the nearest cities.

Two fliers who had not competed in the 1919 air race—but played an important part in it nevertheless—were among the first to become bush-flying legends. They were Hudson Fysh and P. J. McGinness, comrades from the Australian Flying Corps. Unable to obtain a plane for the race, they had agreed instead to locate suitable landing sites in the uncharted wilderness of northern Australia, to be used in case any of the contestants completed the flight to Darwin and then flew on across the Outback to Melbourne. Fysh and McGinness conducted the survey

in a Tin Lizzie, making a 1,354-mile trip that took three slogging months.

In the course of their survey, the two young men woke up to the obvious—that aircraft could provide a variety of valuable services for the scattered residents of the Outback. They talked about it with two wealthy graziers, Fergus McMaster and Ainslie Templeton, who agreed to back them, and in 1921 the aviators launched a bush air service using two war-surplus biplanes. One was an Avro 504K, a large-winged, easy-to-fly trainer powered by a 100-horsepower engine. The other was a 90-horsepower BE-2E reconnaissance craft.

The Avro could carry two passengers and the old BE-2E one. Both flew at a sedate 65 miles per hour. Fysh and McGinness called their venture the Queensland and Northern Territory Aerial Service, or Qantas, and based themselves at the rough frontier town of Longreach, in the heart of Queensland's sheep country.

Before it became anything like a legitimate airline, Qantas had to fight for its financial survival. During the first year, Fysh and McGinness visited much of Queensland, gaining publicity by giving joy rides at a hefty three pounds a head—or five pounds if they looped the loop. One of their first customers was the manager of a sheep station who hired the BE-2E to hunt wild brush turkeys. While pilot Fysh skimmed low over the flat scrub where the birds fed, his passenger blasted away from the front seat with a shotgun. He bagged several turkeys, which stockmen retrieved and carried back to the station.

Hudson Fysh (left), cofounder of the Queensland and Northern Territory Aerial Service, or Qantas, and the company's engineer, Arthur Baird, stand proudly before their BE-2E after the first Qantas flight across the wilderness from Sydney in the south to Winton in the north. Divided into 10 short stages, the 1,200-mile journey took 17½ hours' flying time to complete.

Fysh dangles an Australian scrub turkey shot from the air by the manager (left) of a Queensland sheep station, or ranch. When the owner of the station found out about the aerial hunt, he registered his disapproval of the unsporting practice by firing the manager on the spot.

Living conditions in the Outback, the men knew, could be as rough as the small clearings and potholed pastures they flew from, but the pilots were not prepared for what they found at one town. After a long day of giving joy rides, Fysh and his mechanic were surprised to see smoke coming from the doors of the hotel they expected to stay in. "We discovered," Fysh later wrote, "that it came from smouldering cow dung that had been put in the rooms in defense against the mosquitoes. There was no spare accommodation for us; the beer was hot; fights were going on; even the dogs were having it out in the street." Despite the uproar, the two aviators bedded down and slept under the hotel's billiard table.

Many of Qantas' early customers had never seen an airplane until they rode in one, and a few isolated ranchers, it was said, had not even heard of the Wright brothers' invention. Fysh loved to tell the story of how he once swooped into a remote sheep station and was greeted by a humble grazier holding his hat in hand and mumbling, "Hello, God, my name is Smith."

While Fysh and McGinness barnstormed Queensland in an effort to make Qantas a going concern, another resourceful aviator, named Norman Brearley, was building up a similar bush-flying service 2,000 miles to the west across deserts that rivaled the Gobi and Sahara. Like Qantas' founders, Brearley was a veteran of the War, having worked his passage from Australia to England in 1915 and joined the RFC. By mid-1916 he was flying de Havilland 2 pusher-engined fighter planes over the battlefield at Ypres. His combat tour ended when he was shot down in no man's land, where he hid in a shell hole until rescued after dark by British soldiers. When he recovered from his wounds, he became an instructor at an advanced training base. The extra skill he developed there would be invaluable in his bush-flying days.

In 1918, the War over, Brearley purchased two surplus Avros in England, put them in crates and shipped them to Australia. Brearley followed soon after, landing at Fremantle. Like Fysh and McGinness, he perceived that the plane could be the answer to the problems posed by his native land's sparsely settled interior. He headed for Perth, where he had attended the Technical College before the War. There he began barnstorming in August 1919 in an effort to convince the people of Western Australia that aircraft were not only useful but also safe.

Brearley came close to proving the opposite on his first flight, when, in front of a large crowd, he took the Mayor of Perth for a ride over the city. As he came in to land at the East Perth Oval, home of a cricket club and the only suitable field, Brearley failed to avoid a power line. "I cleared the electric wires with the wheels but felt the plane buck as the tailskid caught," he later wrote. "The plane jerked momentarily. Then the electric light wires broke. We sailed down to make a short landing which distorted the undercarriage slightly." Fortunately the mayor had not noticed the near disaster and shook the relieved pilot by the hand, thanking him for the most enjoyable new experience.

Blessed with mayoral approval, Brearley's two-plane bush outfit was soon in business. Brearley did anything and everything to keep the planes flying: performing aerobatics at race meetings, giving flying lessons, flying newsmen in search of a scoop. On one such occasion, when the Prince of Wales visited Perth in 1920, Brearley and a steel-nerved reporter flew only feet above the royal train for 40 miles. Later the Prince thanked the pilot for providing his first "flying escort."

Soon Brearley was flying charters up and down Australia's sparsely populated west coast, ranging north and south from Perth, and also penetrating the Outback. The interior was even more forbidding than in Queensland. Sheep stations were separated by desert and scrub so savage that the settlers had imported Afghan camels to pack supplies across the arid wastes. Brearley worked out a simple signal system with the graziers in the remote interior stations. If they wanted one of his planes to land for any reason, they would spread a bed sheet on the ground. The sheet was also supposed to indicate a good, level landing place, but it often turned out that what a station manager thought was a suitable runway proved to be pocked with holes or booby-trapped with soft, sandy areas. Either would catch a plane's undercarriage and upend the machine. Brearley also found that cattle would often eat the fabric off the wings, attracted by the aroma of banana oil in the lacquer.

To help cope with emergencies, he applied to the government for permission to carry field telegraphs on his planes, and received it. When mishaps occurred or when planes were forced down by storms or mechanical failure, the pilots could send calls for help by hooking their transmitters to the government telegraph line that crossed the Outback.

Brearley's big break came in 1921, when he won a government contract—worth £25,000 a year—to operate a mail service linking the

Barnstormer Charlie Pratt awaits customers at an impromptu airfield in the Outback, Australia's dusty interior. By giving joy rides to Bushies, as the Outback's settlers were called, Pratt and other early Australian aviators helped awaken the public to the airplane's potential for bridging the continent's enormous distances.

west coast's scattered fishing and pearling settlements. His weekly service ran from Geraldton—200 miles north of Perth, at the end of the rail line—to Derby, about 1,200 miles farther up the coast. Brearley re-equipped his company, now known as Western Australian Airways, with six Bristol Tourer biplanes, modified World War I fighters. Powered by 240-horsepower Siddeley Puma engines, they could carry two passengers each, plus 100 pounds of mail, at 100 miles an hour. The water-cooled engines, designed for the European climate, had a disconcerting habit of boiling over in the torrid Australian summer sun, but Brearley overcame this drawback by schooling his pilots in the art of nursing the aircraft slowly up to higher and cooler cruising altitudes.

Brearley also hired four war-veteran pilots: Len Taplin, Bob Fawcett, H. A. Blake, Val Abbott and a young daredevil from Brisbane named Charles Kingsford-Smith who, after his apprenticeship as a bush flier, would become famous as the first aviator, with copilot Charles Ulm, to fly the Pacific Ocean. On December 5, 1921, three of the Bristols took off, amid a blaze of publicity, on the inaugural run, with Taplin, Fawcett and Brearley at the controls.

They had flown less than 100 miles when engine trouble forced Taplin to make an emergency landing in a forbidding area of sand and scrub a few miles from a large sheep station. Moments later Bob Faw-

After arriving by sea from Perth, one of Norman Brearley's World War I-surplus Avro training planes is towed past the general store in the Western

Australia town of Carnarvon. The aircraft was on its way to the local racecourse for reassembly and takeoff.

cett, in the second plane, arrived on the scene, flying at low level. Apparently more concerned with watching the crippled aircraft than his own air speed, Fawcett slowed down, stalled, then spun into the ground. The pilot and his mechanic, Edward Broad, were killed.

Brearley landed in a clearing a few miles from the spot where the first plane had gone down. Two aboriginal stockmen galloped over on horseback with the news that Fawcett's plane had crashed. Brearley and one of his two passengers borrowed the stockmen's horses and rode over to Taplin's plane to find that a misfiring engine had forced him down. He had not been hurt and soon had the engine running again. After burying Fawcett and Broad near the crash site, Brearley and Taplin flew to Perth to report the details of the accident.

Despite this tragic beginning, Brearley managed to get the mail service running efficiently, and although hindered by Australia's unpredictable weather and roughhewn airstrips, his planes flew 250,000 miles without further accident in the first 18 months of service. Still, there were setbacks. While doing an aerial survey to improve the mail route, Brearley and Kingsford-Smith, accompanied by mechanic Peter Hansen, were forced by a broken oil line to land on a beach south of the pearling

Norman Brearley (center) and pilots of his fledgling Western Australian Airways, including Charles Kingsford-Smith (far left), show off one of the line's new Bristol biplanes. Besides carrying passengers and cargo, W.A.A. offered, as Brearley proudly noted, "the first regular and frequent deliveries of the mail to small townships along the northwestern coast."

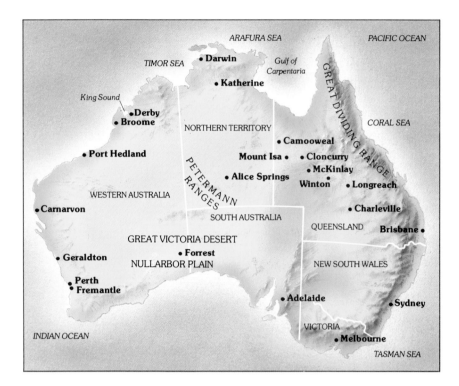

ARAFURA SEA · PACIFIC OCEAN · TIMOR SEA · • Darwin · Gulf of Carpentaria · GREAT DIVIDING RANGE · • Katherine · King Sound · • Derby · • Broome · CORAL SEA · NORTHERN TERRITORY · • Camooweal · • Port Hedland · Mount Isa • · • Cloncurry · • McKinlay · PETERMANN RANGES · • Alice Springs · Winton • · • Longreach · WESTERN AUSTRALIA · • Carnarvon · • Charleville · SOUTH AUSTRALIA · QUEENSLAND · Brisbane • · GREAT VICTORIA DESERT · • Forrest · NULLARBOR PLAIN · NEW SOUTH WALES · • Geraldton · • Perth · • Fremantle · • Adelaide · • Sydney · INDIAN OCEAN · VICTORIA · • Melbourne · TASMAN SEA

Australia, the largest island and at the same time the smallest continent in the world, is sparsely settled throughout its enormous Outback. There, dust storms and occasional downpours made early bush flying a treacherous business.

settlement of Broome. They could not fly out, so Hansen set off on foot for a telegraph line that he knew lay 14 miles away; his plan was to tap the wires and send an SOS with a telegrapher's key he carried for emergencies. On the way, however, he stumbled upon a sheep station. The owner accompanied him to the nearest telegraph office, where they notified authorities in Broome. Since a relief plane could not safely land on the soft sand, a boat was dispatched. After two days, the pilots were rescued, suffering from heat exhaustion and sunburn.

Back in eastern Australia Fysh and McGinness, in 1922, stole a page from Norman Brearley's book and secured a mail contract for Qantas. It called for a regular schedule of runs linking the interior Queensland sheep towns of Charleville, Longreach and Cloncurry. Fysh was able to acquire a pair of Armstrong Whitworth FK 8 biplanes that could carry two passengers as well as the mail and odd items of freight. The planes were slow, cruising at 70 miles an hour, and the open-cockpit passenger accommodations were far from luxurious: Qantas supplied helmets and goggles for each traveler. But between the mail subsidy and the passenger fares, the tiny air service was financially viable at last.

The first passenger on Qantas' 310-mile Longreach-to-Cloncurry section was an 87-year-old grazier named Alexander Kennedy. Excited by the idea of an air service, he had become one of the company's earliest investors. At the end of the four-and-a-half-hour flight, Kennedy recalled that when he had first made the same trip 53 years earlier in an oxcart it had taken eight months.

Committed now to regular service, weather permitting, Qantas had to put new emphasis on plane maintenance. Arthur Baird, the chief engineer, virtually lived in the company's Longreach hangar, trying to keep the tiny fleet of canvas-and-wire planes in flying trim. Baird's apparently instinctive affinity for aero engines and airframes extended, it turned out, to flying as well. When the old BE-2E became so worn that it was uneconomical to operate, Baird was told to burn it. But satisfied that it was good for a few more flights, he climbed in and began teaching himself to fly. Having thus demonstrated his ability, he was formally trained by the company. Thereafter he often acted as a relief pilot.

Despite the emphasis on maintenance, occasional breakdowns were inevitable. One Qantas pilot was forced to land with a broken crankshaft on a stony ridge 250 miles from base. A second aircraft located the downed machine and flew in a replacement engine and a mechanic. With the mechanic's help, the two aviators changed the 500-pound engines; the temperature was more than 120°, and tools had to be submerged in a bucket of water to cool them off. For lifting equipment, they strung a block and tackle between three iron posts "borrowed" from a nearby telegraph line. They completed the job in a day.

Although Qantas operated scheduled mail and passenger services, it remained basically a bush operation throughout the 1920s, flying many mercy missions that anticipated Australia's remarkable Flying Doctor Service, which brought medical care to every corner of the Outback on a regular basis after its inception in 1928. Hudson Fysh vividly recalled an early medical mission. It occurred during the Wet of 1924, one of the worst on record, when the Queensland countryside became a vast lake. On February 21, he was asked to rescue a Mrs. Armstrong, wife of the manager of a sheep station, who was about to have a baby and needed to be rushed to a hospital. Weather conditions were wretched, and Fysh

Before a flight in Qantas' open-cockpit D.H.4, Hudson Fysh buttons a passenger in an overcoat to protect her from chill winds aloft. Such solicitude ended on takeoff. "Who amongst the pilots worried about passengers in those days?" Fysh said years later. "Almost every one of them got sick."

A Bristol Tourer, one of the six owned by Western Australian Airways, attracts a crowd of curious onlookers as mechanics check the undercarriage. Flying between ports on the western coast of Australia, W.A.A. prospered in spite of fares two to three times those charged by steamers.

worried that Mrs. Armstrong might give birth in the air. Yet the flight had to be tried: Fysh had learned, as he later wrote, "that some years before, when no airplanes were available, Mr. Armstrong's first wife was due to have a baby. Down came the floods, cutting them off from medical help, and mother and child died. Mr. Armstrong had married again and now the same dread position had arisen."

Stifling his fears, Fysh flew to the station in the old BE-2E, landing on a road that was still firm enough, and lifted Mrs. Armstrong into the passenger seat in front. Safe at the hospital, she gave birth to a girl.

On many of its medical missions, Qantas ferried the pioneer flying physician of Australia, Dr. Frederic A. Hope Michod, to remote sheep stations. Dr. Michod, quick to see the advantages offered by aircraft in Australia, had been an early investor (of £250) in Qantas and was the first doctor to visit patients in the Outback by plane. Hudson Fysh recalled one occasion in 1925 when the doctor wished to take a crippled woman from his own small hospital at Longreach to a larger medical facility in far-off Brisbane. The first part of the journey would be by air, from Longreach to Charleville; there, the woman could be transferred to a train that would carry her the remaining 400 miles to Brisbane.

The best Qantas plane for the mission was a de Havilland 50; it had an enclosed cabin with space for a stretcher. Unfortunately, the aircraft had not yet returned from an earlier mission, leaving only a smaller D.H.9C with open cockpits to carry Dr. Michod's patient. Because the woman could hardly move, she would have to be lifted into the plane. This job fell to chief mechanic Arthur Baird, who suspended a block and tackle in the doorway of Qantas' Longreach hangar. The woman was placed on a seat and hoisted into the air. The plane was then swung around underneath her so that she could be lowered into the cockpit. When the flight was over, she was extracted in the same manner.

These informal if frequent mercy flights were put on an organized basis by the Most Reverend John Flynn, superintendent of the Presbyterian Church's Australian Inland Mission, and founder of its soon-to-be-famous Flying Doctor Service. Flynn first established a medical facility and flying headquarters at Cloncurry. He then signed an agreement calling for Qantas to provide a plane and pilot to fly physicians from the clinic to isolated settlements. Flynn next set about providing every ranch and settlement with a radio sending set that could flash a distress signal to Cloncurry when an emergency arose. At first the sets were simple Morse code transmitters powered by pedal generators. Later Flynn's organization invented and distributed typewriter-like sending sets that enabled a grazier to spell out his message.

Flynn's ambition, in the words of the motto he proposed for the service, was to throw "A Mantle of Safety" over the Outback. This he did, although for several years the service employed only one physician, Dr. St. Vincent Welch, one Qantas de Havilland 50 and a single pilot. In its first year of operation, 1928, the de Havilland covered no less than 17,479 miles. By the time Qantas turned over the flying duties to Trans-

Australia Airlines 19 years later, John Flynn's great experiment was operating hospitals, clinics and air bases all over the Outback. In 1955, the service received a charter from England's Queen Elizabeth that added the word "Royal" to its name. By then, it was flying hundreds of patients a year from nearly 1,200 outposts to 12 medical centers around the country. It had, as one Australian noted, changed "the face of two million square miles," defeating the psychological terror of the Outback's remoteness and alleviating the very real fear of its physical dangers. The Royal Flying Doctor Service was the first of its kind in the world and remains invaluable to this day.

Once bush pilots had become an accepted part of Outback life, they found themselves performing all kinds of odd aerial errands. On Christmas morning, 1927, Qantas' Arthur Affleck, who often flew medical missions, received an urgent summons to the town of Camooweal, little more than a crossroads in the Queensland Outback. Thieves had capped a series of robberies in the town with the theft of a new car. By the time a citizen discovered tire tracks leading south out of town, the thieves had a 12-hour head start. So the people of Camooweal swiftly pooled their cash and telegraphed Affleck to fly over at once from his base at Cloncurry. What followed was Australia's first air chase.

Affleck landed at Camooweal a few hours later, paused long enough to enjoy a Christmas dinner, then zoomed off in pursuit of the thieves in his Qantas de Havilland 50, with the town constable, a

A doctor and attendants of the Australian Inland Mission's flying doctor service prepare to transfer an accident victim from a Qantas-supplied de Havilland 50A to an ambulance in Brisbane. There, surgeons were able to save the badly injured legs of the man, who had been flown 1,200 miles from Camooweal, Queensland.

Sergeant Geise, and the owner of the stolen car as passengers.

After a while, Affleck and his passengers passed over a lonely sheep station named Headingley. They landed in an open field to ask if the stolen car had gone by. It had not. Evidently the thieves, having seen or heard the plane, had turned off short of Headingley to hide in the bush. Very possibly they had passed through a gate in the fence that marked the border between Queensland and the Northern Territory—and had escaped beyond Sergeant Geise's jurisdiction. Affleck and his companions parked the plane, borrowed a truck and headed back north, retracing the route they had flown over. Soon they found tire tracks. They followed them to the warm ashes of a small cooking fire.

In hot pursuit now, the three men tracked their quarry until sunset, when they saw the glow of a campfire ahead. They stopped the truck and crept through the brush to find four men around the fire. The dusty stolen car stood nearby, with rifles leaning against it and water bags hanging from the bumper. Drawing revolvers, the pursuers jumped out.

"You're under arrest," Sergeant Geise announced.

"You can't arrest us," rejoined one of the thieves, "we're in the Territory and you're a Queensland constable with no jurisdiction here."

"Quite so," said Geise, "but a Queensland policeman can take possession of property stolen in Queensland." With that, he and his companions scooped up the rifles and water bags—which Geise assumed the car thieves had also stolen during the crime wave at Camooweal—and the three men retreated in the two vehicles. "Now," explained the constable to Affleck as they jounced along in the truck, "we only have to be waiting for them at the nearest water, and that's on the other side of the border fence—in Queensland."

The next day, just as he had predicted, the thieves straggled back into Queensland and headed right for the water hole where Geise and his party were waiting to arrest them. They gave up without a struggle.

Some of Qantas' regular flights turned into adventures of another sort. Eric Donaldson, who had been wounded twice while flying with the RFC and later became chief pilot for the Flying Doctor Service, recalled a phenomenon peculiar to the Outback—the dust storms called "Bedouries." During severe Dry periods, windstorms would whip up huge clouds of dust. The heavier particles would sift to the ground, leaving a nearly impenetrable haze of dust whirling in the air.

Australia's Sugar Bird Lady

"I was born with the sound of aircraft thundering overhead," wrote Robin Miller, nurse, pilot and daughter of famed bush flier Horrie Miller. Miller's father had tried to dissuade her from taking up flying but she earned a commercial license anyway and in 1967 took the first piloting job she could get: delivering oral polio vaccine to 30,000 people scattered across the Outback.

The worst part of the work was landing on the marginal airstrips of the region. One such strip featured a hidden sinkhole deep enough to overturn her Cessna 182. Luckily she missed it. Another curved between sand dunes like a snake.

Administering the vaccine proved to be easier than delivering it. Dripped onto sugar cubes, it was eagerly downed by even the smallest aborigine children, who called Miller the "Sugar Bird Lady."

Having proved her mettle, Miller became a Royal Flying Doctor Service pilot in 1969. Her career, however, was cut tragically short. In 1975, she was stricken with cancer and died at the age of 34.

Robin Miller steps from a Beechcraft Baron belonging to the Royal Flying Doctors after helping ferry the plane 11,000 miles from the United States to Australia.

Pilots caught in Bedouries could not see the horizon in the west, where the dust clouds came from, and when facing into the sun were virtually blind. The only way to navigate was to fly at 500 feet or less, leaning out of the cockpit and looking backward, hoping to recognize a landmark.

On a flight from Camooweal to Cloncurry, Donaldson became lost in one of these dust clouds. Unable to locate his usual checkpoint, a settlement called Mount Isa, he found himself over an unfamiliar sheep station. "I flew around, but there was no place to get down so I shut off the engine and glided over the station at very low altitude, and called out 'Where's Isa?' " The sheep station personnel, attracted by the noise of the plane, heard Donaldson's desperate shout. Waving their arms, they pointed the way. Donaldson found Isa, then picked up a rail line, and finally made his way into Cloncurry. His arrival out of the dust cloud, Donaldson noted dryly, "was totally unexpected."

Norman Brearley's Western Australian Airways, like Qantas, increasingly made its money from airmail runs and passenger services. Nevertheless, the air service—now known as West Australian Airways—continued in the 1930s to seek charter assignments. A mission in 1932 was among the most dangerous a West Australian pilot ever undertook. It involved a search for a lost gold strike known as Lasseter's Reef.

The strike was named for an aged prospector, Harold "Possum" Lasseter, who claimed to have discovered it back in the 1890s. The reef, or vein, was located, Lasseter said, in a desolate region of the Petermann Range west of the town of Alice Springs, deep in mountainous central Australia. For three decades, Lasseter had vainly sought backing for an expedition to rediscover the gold. Finally, in 1930, a syndicate of Sydney businessmen provided the necessary money. Lasseter set out with several other adventurers, a train of camels and a six-wheeled truck to find his fortune. Soon, however, Lasseter's companions, unable to bear the heat, turned back in the truck. Lasseter went on with the camels and disappeared; a search party subsequently found his remains.

In December 1932, about two years after Lasseter's demise, two of Perth's leading citizens, a banker and a lawyer, approached Brearley. They wanted to charter a pilot and a D.H.50 for a secret mission. Brearley insisted on knowing what it was. When he learned that the goal was Lasseter's Reef, he wisely demanded a hefty deposit, having little faith that gold would be found and a lively sense that the flights in and out of the central wasteland would be perilous. The pilot Brearley chose for the mission was one of his most experienced, Harry Baker.

Baker took off from Perth in late December—during the summer Dry—carrying a prospector named Paddy Whelan and a mining engineer named Stuckey. They flew 700 miles to Forrest, a tiny outpost in the middle of the vast Nullarbor Plain, which runs along the southern coast between the eastern and western segments of the country. Baker then set out with his passengers to fly 400 miles northeastward across the Great Victoria Desert and the Mann Ranges to the vicinity of Alice

Longreach—Brisbane in 10 Hours.

Modern Travel this—and as SAFE and COMFORTABLE as it is FAST.
Try it—you will agree it is the "ONLY WAY."
THE AIRLINERS 'APOLLO' or 'DIANA,' leave LONGREACH
every SUNDAY at 5.30 a.m. calling at BLACKALL, TAMBO,
CHARLEVILLE, ROMA and TOOWOOMBA, arriving BRISBANE at
3.30 p.m. the same day. THE RETURN TRIP is carried out on
TUESDAYS, BRISBANE being left at 5.30 a.m. and LONGREACH
reached at 3.30 p.m. the same day.

REDUCED FARES

Longreach—Charleville   £6/13/   Longreach—Toowoomba   £13/5/
Longreach—Roma   £8/16/6   Longreach—Brisbane   £14/16/

FULL INFORMATION FROM—

Q.A.N.T.A.S. LTD., LONGREACH.

Agents for AUSTRALIAN NATIONAL AIRWAYS, Brisbane, Sydney,
Melbourne and Perth.

Qantas passengers enjoy morning tea inside a hangar housing a D.H.83 Fox Moth used by Australia's Flying Doctor Service. This picture was taken in 1937,

...ten years after the inset advertisement was created. By then, Qantas had grown from a bush operation into a major airline.

Springs. He planned to leave Whelan and Stuckey there while he returned to Forrest. He would then fly back a few days later to take the two men out—along with any gold they might have found.

It did not work out that way. On the inward flight, while over the Great Victoria Desert, the plane's oil pipe burst, forcing Baker to land. He chose to put down on a solid-looking salt lake. The wheels sank through the surface crust of the dry lake, and the plane stood on its nose, shattering the propeller, then flipped over onto its back, cracking various wooden ribs and struts. Baker, who had been strapped into his cockpit, was unhurt, but Stuckey, the engineer, had fallen out and hit his head on a bracing wire, causing a painful but superficial gash. The prospector, Whelan, had also pitched out of the plane, injuring his hip.

The only shade the three men could find was under a scrawny desert oak. Even there, the temperature was nearly 130°. Baker mended the plane's broken struts as best he could, using branches from the desert's stunted trees as splints and lashing a sapling to the cracked lower wing spar as reinforcement. Baker carried a spare propeller in the plane, but try as they might, he and his companions could not rock the craft back onto its landing gear so that the new prop could be attached. Soon provisions began to peter out. Drinking water became scarce, and attempts to purify some water from salty puddles with an improvised condenser made from a fuel can came to nothing.

On December 27, a breeze sprang up, rocking the de Havilland. The men ran to her and, with the help of the wind, at last managed to tip

The D.H.50A used in the search for Lasseter's Reef bakes in the desert sun after flipping over when its wheels broke through the crust of a dried-up salt lake. Once it was righted and repaired, the plane took off across the lake, threatening to nose over several times before finally becoming airborne.

Pilot Harry Baker (left) stands with mining engineer N. S. Stuckey before fetching his second passenger, prospector Paddy Whelan, from the salt lake. "You put him there; you get him out," was the taunt of an official when Baker asked for government aid in Whelan's rescue. Later the authorities relented and dropped food and water to Whelan.

the plane onto its nose, then onto the landing gear. Baker bolted on the propeller and succeeded in starting the motor.

The lake bed was so soft that Baker realized he would not be able to lift off with both passengers aboard. He left Whelan sitting under the scrub oak and took off with Stuckey. As they headed south to get help, all seemed well until Baker noticed that the fabric on the wing had begun to peel. Evidently he had not sewed the torn spots carefully enough. Stuckey also saw the flapping fabric. Without a word, the 60-year-old engineer climbed out on the lower wing. Grasping a strut to keep from being blown away by the slip stream, he stuffed his undershirt into the hole, stopping the flapping and keeping the fabric from ripping any farther. He then made his way back into the cockpit.

Baker landed first at the hamlet of Cook, a stop on the transcontinental Perth-to-Adelaide railway line, where the onlookers were astonished to see a pair of dirty, unshaven men climb out of the plane, Stuckey with a filthy, bloodstained bandage wrapped around his head. After sending off telegrams announcing their survival, Baker and Stuckey flew on to Forrest and quickly began organizing the rescue of Paddy Whelan.

Despite his exhaustion, Baker volunteered to guide a first relief plane to the parched lake bed. Food and a drum of water were parachuted down, addressed to "Paddy Whelan, Salt Lake City." Baker then insisted that he fly in to rescue the prospector, since only he knew how to land on the treacherous surface of the dried lake. On January 5, 1933, nine days after leaving Whelan behind, he took off from Forrest, found the lake bed once again and made a perfect landing on its rim. Whelan was still there, sitting under the oak, weakened but alive. After Whelan had been helped into the plane, Baker took off and made it back to Forrest without incident. The pilot became something of a national hero. Newspaper headlines in Perth trumpeted BAKER GETS HIS MAN, congratulatory telegrams poured in and a private benefactor presented the aviator with a check for £100. But Brearley, from the perspective of years of bush experience, simply noted: "So ended another unsuccessful search for Lasseter's Lost Reef. No doubt there will be others."

By this time Brearley's West Australian Airways was already well on the way to becoming a full-fledged airline, flying passengers across the Nullarbor Plain from Perth to Adelaide in de Havilland Hercules trimotors, for the first time bridging the continent by air. But after the Depression spread to Australia, W.A.A. foundered, going under in 1936.

In the meantime, Qantas, which had been operating solely in the bush, had added a new route, from its old Charleville base to Brisbane. In February 1935 the company went international when a new four-engined D.H.86, dubbed the *Melbourne,* made its maiden flight to Singapore, where it linked up with Britain's Imperial Airways. For the first time, passengers and mail could go by air from Australia to England. Former Prime Minister Hughes, still a vociferous champion of air travel for Australia, saw the promise of his air race abundantly fulfilled.

Two of the pioneer bush outfits had become true airlines, but a host of independent operators continued to fly the lonely reaches of the Outback. One of the most eccentric was a one-legged pilot with the unusual name of Goya Henry. For a number of years Henry ran a one-man, one-plane joy-ride and charter service in New South Wales. In 1936 he decided to expand into an interstate service, flying from New South Wales to Victoria. But his record of combative independence worked against him: The civil aviation authorities refused to grant him the necessary licenses. With a resourcefulness bred in the Outback, Henry figured that he needed a license only to *fly* across the state borders. So he beat the bureaucrats by landing on border roads, taxiing across the border itself, then gleefully taking off again for his destination.

Just as independent as Goya Henry were Charles Kingsford-Smith, who had gained his bush-flying experience on Norman Brearley's early mail runs, and Charles Ulm, copilot on his pathbreaking transit of the Pacific in 1928. In the same year, they decided to form Australian National Airways, a grand title for a four-plane service linking the cities on Australia's east coast. Equipped with four Avro 10s, a British version of the famed trimotor transport designed by Dutchman Anthony Fokker, the two set themselves the audacious task of keeping to a regular schedule between Brisbane and Sydney whatever the weather.

It was a foolhardy scheme. Aircraft of the day still lacked the ability to climb above high-stacked thunderheads, and the predictable consequence of this deficiency came on the very first day of service, on a flight from Brisbane to Sydney. Ulm, flying south with eight passengers in a plane he and Kingsford-Smith had named *Southern Sky,* ran into monsoon storms that he could not climb above. So he decided to fly under them. Luckily he broke through the overcast in a valley of the McPherson Range, which parallels the coast. He had little choice but to attempt a landing. For all he knew, the valley was a dead end, and climbing back into the clouds would surely result in crashing against a mountainside. Searching the valley's more or less level floor, Ulm spotted a two-acre paddock next to a farmhouse. The farmer, sensing that the plane circling above was in distress, displayed remarkable presence of mind. He instructed his daughter to mount a horse and, trailing a white cloth behind, ride around the perimeter of the small clearing to give Ulm a better sense of the space he had available. Only this unexpected aid and his great flying skill enabled Ulm to get the trimotor safely down.

The forced landing, which compelled the passengers to complete the journey to Sydney by car and train, was a humiliating setback. To recoup some pride, if nothing else, Kingsford-Smith decided to put his bush-flying experience to work and fly the *Southern Sky* out of the clearing. Ignoring demands from the authorities to dismantle the craft and have it hauled out by truck, he brought in a new engine from Brisbane to replace the damaged one and repaired the undercarriage.

He then stripped the plane of all unnecessary gear to lighten it and positioned it at the edge of the woods bordering the farm. There he tied the tail to a tree with a stout hawser so that he could gun the three

The Australian National Airways' plane Southern Sky stands where it came to an abrupt halt after pilot Charles Ulm managed to clear the wooded hill in the background and land in a farmer's pasture. Remarked an undaunted passenger: "It was a superb landing in terrible country, in worst weather and wretched visibility. It was a wonderful advertisement for Australian National Airways."

engines to full power before starting to roll. When the engines were roaring, he gave a signal, a local woodsman hacked the rope with an ax and the big plane lurched forward. As Kingsford-Smith roared across the field, he pulled back on the stick and the Avro leaped into the air, scraped the treetops, cleared the hills and headed for Brisbane.

Australian National Airways survived the publicity of this disaster and doggedly continued to fly through the worst kinds of weather. For a year there were no accidents, then a second Avro, the *Southern Cloud*, was lost in a storm between Sydney and Melbourne, crashing in a mountainous area so remote that the remains of the craft and its eight passengers were not found for 27 years. The loss of the plane ended the Kingsford-Smith and Ulm operation. Soon the famous fliers were gone, too. Returning from England to Australia in a Lockheed Altair, Kingsford-Smith vanished over the Bay of Bengal in 1935. Ulm had run out of fuel on a flight to Hawaii and disappeared into the Pacific a year earlier.

Bush flying continued unabated in Australia throughout the 1930s. If airlines now linked the major cities, there were still regions of the Outback that no scheduled outfit could ever economically service—and tasks only small planes able to land almost anywhere could perform. For example, a much-admired bush pilot of the era was Jack Treacy, who made it his business to battle his way around the Outback delivering movie film. Every little settlement had a cinema, usually just four tin walls and an array of canvas chairs under the stars. The weekly film Treacy delivered was the highlight of the otherwise dull bush routine.

World War II caused a temporary decline in bush operations as the country looked to its survival. Even the Flying Doctor Service had to ration its pilots and planes. But in the postwar years, a new wave of ex-military pilots restored bush flying to vitality. One such aviator was ex-Royal Australian Air Force Pilot Bob Norman. On a damp night in 1951 when all Queensland was awash in the tropical rainy season, word of a life-or-death emergency reached the airfield at Cairns, a coastal town north of Brisbane: At Cargoon, a remote cattle station, the wife of a grazier named Bev Anning was hemorrhaging seriously after a miscarriage. The station was so waterlogged that the large de Havilland Rapide of the Cairns Aerial Ambulance Service could not land there, and neither could Norman, who happened to be at the airport when the emergency call came in. But at Reedy Springs, 10 miles away, was a well-drained slope that might be dry enough for his Tiger Moth to set down on.

Anning set off for Reedy Springs with his wife, Vera, and four station hands in a truck. The journey across the soggy terrain took 36 hours. Anning and his men then had to clear a runway of sorts on the slope. This enabled Norman to land his plane, but Vera Anning, though nearly unconscious from loss of blood, refused to get in. She demanded proof that the plane could take off from the hill with two people inside. Against his better judgment, Norman was persuaded to demonstrate that all would be well by taking Bev Anning for a short spin. Satisfied of her safety, Vera allowed herself to be helped aboard and Norman flew her to the hospital at nearby Hughenden, where transfusions saved her life.

Anning was so grateful and so impressed by Norman's performance that he gladly backed the pilot in a business venture—an air service that would fly in the far northern sections of Queensland and the bushlands of the Cape York Peninsula. With £300 from Anning and like sums from other Outback graziers, Norman created Bush Pilots Airways, initially equipped with one plane, a de Havilland Dragonfly. BPA quickly expanded as demand for all kinds of air services multiplied. Rich mineral deposits were found in northern Queensland and mining towns mushroomed. So did the tourist trade to the coastline's superb beaches and the fishing grounds of the Great Barrier Reef.

Soon Norman and BPA were operating a fleet of 11 British-made Auster Autocars, workhorse aircraft able to lift their own empty weight in payload. Through the 1960s, BPA added a number of single-engined Cessnas to its stable of planes, and in the 1970s, it bought several old but spotless Douglas DC-3s—the sure mark in the postwar era that a bush operation had acquired the stature of a small airline. Today Bush Pilots Airways—known as Air Queensland—maintains service to some 100 tiny airports and grass strips, and its pilots, as others had done for 50 years before them, brave dust, heat and storms to bring necessities and a taste of civilization to the lonely reaches of the continent. ⌇⌇

A spectator, sitting near the spot where the Southern Sky had to become airborne or crash into a wall of trees, watches the plane rev up for takeoff.

3

The challenge of New Guinea

Prime Minister Billy Hughes's great air race from England to Australia in 1919 not only spurred the growth of Australian aviation; the epic competition was indirectly responsible for the birth of bush flying in New Guinea, the huge island to the north. The only men besides winners Keith and Ross Smith to finish the race were two members of Britain's Royal Flying Corps: a diminutive, sharp-featured Australian aviator named Raymond Parer and a towering Scot named John McIntosh, who had been invited along to handle planning and logistics for the flight while Parer looked to the plane and the flying. And it was Ray Parer—building on the experience he gained from his gallant second-place finish—who became the best known of all the pioneer bush pilots who flew in New Guinea, opening up that savage and then largely unexplored tropical island to the modern world.

Parer and McIntosh entered the England-Australia air race in a decrepit de Havilland 9 bomber that they had purchased with £900 given them by Peter Dawson, a Scottish whisky baron who asked in return only that they hand-deliver a bottle of his finest spirits to Prime Minister Hughes. The war-surplus D.H.9, which had sat for months in the open, was in such sad shape that it took Parer and McIntosh weeks to make it even marginally airworthy. By the time they were ready to take off, the Smiths had already arrived at Darwin and the race was officially over. But that did not stop Parer, who was determined to fly to Australia in any case. The ensuing trip became far more a test of will than speed.

Taking off in January 1920, Parer and McIntosh managed to cross Europe in their asthmatic machine. But thereafter the de Havilland broke down with maddening regularity, stranding the pair in forgotten corners of the globe where they had to scrimp, scrounge and improvise in order to get the plane going again. Forced down in the deserts of the Middle East, they were saved from marauding bandits only by a hand grenade that McIntosh had thoughtfully brought along. When the airmen ran out of cash for food and fuel, they raised money by turning the plane into a flying billboard. Obliged by engine trouble to land on a Burmese riverbank, they cajoled local residents into hacking an airstrip

At a New Guinea airstrip in 1930, workers gather by the Junkers W 33 that bush pilot Ray Parer (left) and his brother Kevin (right) used to ferry miners to gold fields in the island's forbidding interior.

from the jungle so they could take off after making repairs. Still in Burma, they crashed and had to rebuild their machine. They battled tropical squalls and countless other obstacles that would have daunted lesser men. Fabric peeled off the wings and fires erupted in midflight, but miraculously the pair survived.

For 208 days they struggled on until finally they sputtered across the shark-infested Timor Sea from the East Indies (present-day Indonesia) to Australia and arrived over Darwin on August 2, 1920. As they came to the end of their landing run, the engine consumed the last drop of fuel and stopped dead as a welcoming crowd, cheering tumultuously, surged around them. Parer and McIntosh were national heroes. The Australians, with their love of the odd man out, took the bad-luck duo to their hearts, and the government awarded them each a consolation prize of £500 for their courage and determination.

McIntosh had little time to enjoy his celebrity; he was killed in an airplane accident on Easter, 1921. But for Parer, the flight was the first of many exploits that earned him the nickname Battling Parer. In Australian slang, a battler is someone who encounters endless misfortune and long odds but nevertheless carries on with a grin—and who always helps his "mates" despite his own troubles. It was a sobriquet of distinction in that tough land and Parer bore it the rest of his life.

Early in 1921 Parer bought an FE-2B pusher biplane to go barnstorming in. A few months later, during a round-Australia tour, he snagged his plane on a telegraph wire and plunged into a butcher's wagon on the main street of Kalgoorlie. Parer was not seriously injured, but his plane was wrecked beyond salvage, and with so many war-trained pilots roaming Australia, he could not find a permanent flying job. So he gave up aviation and moved to tiny King Island, off the southern coast of Australia near Tasmania, where he earned a livelihood by running a small garage.

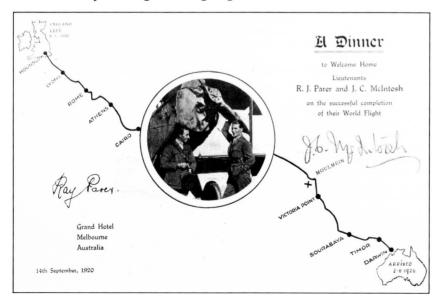

Ray Parer, John McIntosh and the D.H.9 they flew from England to Australia in 1920 are featured on a souvenir menu from a dinner honoring them in Melbourne, their final destination. After their plane crash-landed 200 miles north of the city, it had to be dismantled and shipped by freight train on the last leg of the journey.

In 1925, word reached King Island of a magnificent gold find in New Guinea. Navigators coasting New Guinea had for nearly 100 years reported seeing ferocious-looking tribesmen decorated with raw nuggets, and a few intrepid prospectors had penetrated its jungles to stake claims. Then in 1922 a legendary prospector, William "Shark-Eye" Park—so named for his cold and penetrating stare—discovered rich deposits in Koranga Creek, a swift-flowing tributary of the Bulolo River 40 miles inland from New Guinea's northeastern coast. Park tried to keep his discovery secret, but rumors spread and by the time Parer heard of it, about 50 of Australia's most hardened prospectors had rushed to New Guinea by ship and debarked at the tiny settlements of Lae and Salamaua. From there they scrambled up the sides of mountains and through dense jungles to stake more claims and pan for gold on the Bulolo and its various tributaries, the richest of which turned out to be Edie Creek.

Battling Parer saw immediately that airplanes were the only solution to the transportation problems faced by the prospectors. News filtering out of New Guinea indicated that it could take a miner and his train of pack bearers 10 days to struggle the 35 miles from the coastal villages to the gold fields. Building a road or laying railway tracks through such rugged country would be prohibitively expensive. Parer pooled his resources with a farmer by the name of Eric Gallet who was bored with raising sugar cane and wanted adventure. They purchased a used de Havilland 4, a World War I biplane bomber, and flew it to Sydney. Their plan was to ship the aircraft to Rabaul on New Britain Island, north of New Guinea—a direct Australia-New Guinea flight was too long—and then fly from Rabaul to Lae, where a primitive airstrip was under construction.

It was on the Sydney docks that Parer met face to face the aviator who would become his great rival in New Guinea, a fellow veteran named Andrew E. "Pard" (for pardner) Mustar.

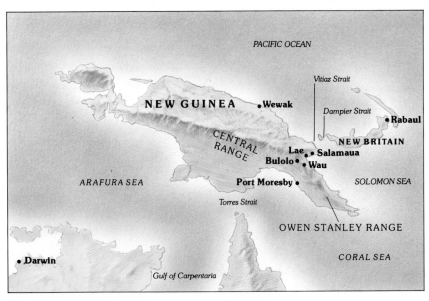

New Guinea presented daunting obstacles to the bush pilots who inaugurated its air routes during the 1920s and 1930s. Fliers had to penetrate mist-shrouded mountains that split the jungle island in two and limited the airstrips carved from the jagged terrain to rough-and-ready affairs that made takeoffs and landings a gamble at best.

Pard Mustar had been employed to take a plane to New Guinea by an Australian-based company formed to extract the gold from Edie Creek. The founders of the firm, called Guinea Gold, had also realized that the rich find could never be developed efficiently without a dependable transportation link to the coast. Porters were slow, expensive and limited by Australian law—northeastern New Guinea was then governed under a League of Nations mandate by Australia—to a load of no more than 50 pounds. Guinea Gold therefore, on December 30, 1926, bought a new government-surplus de Havilland 37 biplane, planning to haul its own men and equipment and to sell the plane's excess capacity to others who needed to reach the interior. Still in the original crate, the D.H.37 had been shipped from England and delivered to the Sydney docks. Accompanying it were Mustar and an expert mechanic, A.W.D. "Mull" Mullins, whose given names are forgotten. Their destination was also Rabaul, where they would uncrate the aircraft and assemble it for their flight to Lae. A race was on to see who could get to New Guinea first—and win the lion's share of the business hauling men and freight to the gold fields.

The odds were not even. The D.H.4 Parer flew had been perhaps the best day bomber produced by either side during World War I, but it had been designed to carry its load of bombs on racks beneath the wings. It had been modified by its previous owner to carry two passengers behind the pilot, but it still offered Parer no proper cargo space within its slim fuselage. Guinea Gold's D.H.37 was a postwar machine designed to carry two passengers or 600 pounds of freight and it was powered by one of the finest aero engines of the day, a Rolls-Royce Falcon of 275 horsepower. Furthermore, Mustar had with him Mull Mullins, while Parer's partner, Eric Gallet, was a farmer and not an airplane mechanic.

Parer had a momentary advantage, however, in the comedy of errors that commenced at once. When Mustar and Mullins arrived at the Sydney docks, they discovered that Parer had forestalled them, taking an option on the only deck space available on the next freighter bound for Rabaul. But when the time came to sail, Parer did not have the cash to pay for his plane's passage. Gleefully, Mustar and Mullins took his place on the freighter, loaded their de Havilland and sailed for New Britain.

Parer, resilient as ever, raised the money to follow on the next ship, hoping to catch up while Mustar and Mullins were assembling their plane in Rabaul. But Parer, who was never meticulous about the condition of his aircraft, had neglected to check the air pressure in the tires. By the time the D.H.4 reached Rabaul they were flat and had been cut by the wheel rims as the ship rolled on the waves. Parer had to have new tires shipped from Australia. To make matters worse, one of the wings was damaged during unloading.

Meanwhile, Mustar and Mullins had reached Rabaul, where they assembled their plane and flight-tested it. On March 30, 1927, having received word by radio that the airstrip at Lae was ready, they took off on the perilous 400-mile flight across the Solomon Sea to New Guinea. They hugged New Britain's north coast as long as they could, then traversed the Dampier and Vitiaz Straits on the one-hour, open-water crossing to New Guinea.

Luck was with them, and four and a half hours out of Rabaul they came to Finschhafen, 75 miles from Lae on the tip of a peninsula. After skimming above the shoreline for another hour, they landed safely at their destination. Miners, who had heard that Mustar was on the way, already were queueing up to be the first to fly to the gold fields.

The trip from Lae to the gold-mining settlement of Wau turned out to be a nightmare of a flight. It began at an airstrip that was only 600 yards long. From the air it looked, Mustar noted, like a "miniature tennis court." Lae was at sea level, but only a short distance inland the terrain rose abruptly to 6,000 feet. A pilot was forced to climb steeply to clear the mountains, often cloaked in cloud, and then almost to dive on Wau, which lay in a valley at 3,200 feet.

It took Mustar several attempts to find the tiny airstrip that had been hacked out of the jungle at Wau. Several prospectors who knew the way on foot volunteered to fly with him and provide directions. But what had been familiar to them on the ground became a baffling maze from the air.

After repeated failures, Mustar recruited yet another miner, a man named Lewers who turned out to have an inexplicable aptitude for aerial navigation. Lewers recognized resting spots he had used on his treks into the mountains and guided Mustar over the shoulders of the coastal range and through a bank of clouds to a cleared strip of land climbing up the side of a grassy valley.

But having found the Wau airstrip did not end Mustar's problems. The cleared area was only 800 yards long and sloped upward at a gradient of 1 in 12. The only possible approach was to fly up the hillside leading to the strip using full power and then turn sharply to land, since the strip was cut at an angle to the slope. Mustar made a wild, yawing turn, pulled off the power and thumped down. After almost flipping the aircraft over on this first landing at Wau, the sweating pilot declared it to be "the world's worst aerodrome."

Meanwhile, in Rabaul, Battling Parer finally received his new tires the day after Mustar's hair-raising baptismal landing at Wau. After repairing the plane's wing, Parer and Gallet took off for a test flight. Pleased with the performance of the machine, Parer came in to land at the Rabaul airfield. But one wheel sank into a soft patch of the field and a wing tip brushed the ground, flipping the biplane onto its back. Parer escaped with cuts and bruises, but Gallet suffered a broken collarbone. To make matters worse, the plane was badly mangled and required extensive repairs. For Gallet this was the last straw. He went back to Australia.

Drawing on the experience he had gained rebuilding the bomber he

Pard Mustar, the first bush pilot in New Guinea, prepares to take off from Lae in his D.H.37, Old Faithful. At the right wing tip, Mustar's partner, Mull Mullins, collects a fare from one of the two passengers that the aircraft could accommodate.

and McIntosh had flown from England to Australia, Parer accomplished the reconstruction in a couple of months and on June 23, 1927, made a successful crossing from Rabaul to Lae, launching his Bulolo Goldfields Aeroplane Service. Miners who worked digs not controlled by Guinea Gold took to him immediately. They recalled his heroic England-Australia flight, and in manner, language and looks he was one of them, a bona fide "digger." With their love for the independent operator, and the underdog, the small-time miners patronized Parer's air service, whenever he was able to fly his cranky plane, rather than the more reliable company-backed service being run by Pard Mustar. If Parer ran short of cash, as he frequently did, the miners loaned him money. They had brought their tradition of "mateship" from the Australian Outback to the jungles of New Guinea.

In addition, Parer quickly undercut Guinea Gold's high fares and freight rates. As a result, Parer always had customers and remained a thorn in the side of his competition.

Nonetheless, Mustar had the advantage. With a more suitable aircraft and his own mechanic to keep it operating, he was soon averaging two trips a day between Lae and Wau. In the first six months he carried 150 passengers and 80,000 pounds of supplies into the crazily canted airstrip at Wau. By then he had mastered its tricky approach and had learned to keep the D.H.37, which had no brakes, from rolling backward down the airstrip after the plane came to a stop. As the aircraft slowed, Mustar simply used the last of its fading momentum to turn sideways on the hill. Chocks placed in front of and behind the wheels ensured that the machine would not move accidentally.

While Parer and Mustar were fighting it out for freight contracts and passengers, more Australian bush pilots were enticed to New Guinea to get in on the action and excitement. Some of them joined Pard Mustar's service and others signed on with Battling Parer. A few went to work for small mining companies that attempted to establish their own airlift operations, but these outfits generally lacked the resources to acquire suitable aircraft. Les Shaw, signed up by the Morobe Trading Company, was provided with a tiny de Havilland Moth, an excellent sport plane but one with a capacity to lift only 350 pounds of freight. Edie Creek Gold Company's pilot, Charles Matheson, brought with him an Avro 504K that the company had purchased. The Avro, whose design dated back to 1914, had been a first-rate World War I trainer, but its cargo capacity was even less than that of Shaw's Moth. Matheson had little chance to assess the shortcomings of his plane, however, for on his first flight from Lae the engine failed and the Avro plunged straight into the sea near the mouth of the Buang River. Matheson and his engineer managed to swim to safety—and took the next ship home to Australia.

Whether bush pilots in New Guinea flew small planes or large ones, they all faced some of the worst flying conditions anywhere on the globe. Australia's Outback may have been vast and often intolerably hot, but it was largely flat. New Guinea had sharp-edged mountains around which sudden and violent storms swirled, often blinding a pilot on his way into the interior and then cutting off his retreat. There were no navigational aids, no emergency landing fields, and the rugged terrain made a successful forced landing improbable at best. In the early years of New Guinea bush flying, the planes did not even carry radios for sending distress calls.

If flying conditions were perilous, living conditions were ghastly. The fever-breeding sultriness of the tropics enveloped New Guinea. Malaria was rampant among gold miners and pilots alike. The aviators' dank bunkhouses were infested with all manner of repellent lizards and stinging insects, and the slovenly couple that operated the airmen's mess at Lae were said to be familiar with only one cooking utensil: a can opener. Perpetual dampness shortened the lives of planes' engines and rotted the fabric from wings, making maintenance difficult and aircraft risky to take up. And downed fliers sometimes had fatal encounters with roving warriors from New Guinea's more remote tribes. The mortality rate among bush pilots in New Guinea far outstripped that of their peers in Australia or Alaska.

While Shaw, Matheson and others suffered with tiny airplanes and struggled, mostly in vain, to gain a toe hold at Lae, Guinea Gold expanded its airlift operation, changing the name to Guinea Airways Ltd. On Mustar's advice, the company purchased an additional aircraft: a husky, powerful, all-metal monoplane made by one of the leading transport plane manufacturers of the late 1920s, Junkers of Germany. When the first Junkers W 34 proved a success, Guinea Airways bought four more. A humpbacked ugly duckling in appearance, the W 34, powered by a 420-horsepower Bristol Jupiter engine, could lift nearly a ton and a half of cargo. Modern aviation technology had at last reached the gold fields, and despite the Junkers' habit of making a wicked swing to the right on touchdown, Pard Mustar and his team of pilots were delighted with the new aircraft.

Parer responded to Guinea Gold's expansion by purchasing two more airplanes. But, short of funds as usual, he had to be content with a D.H.9C—an improved two-passenger version of his D.H.4—and a civilian conversion of a Bristol Fighter. Taking delivery of the planes in Port Moresby on the southern New Guinea coast, he undertook to fly them to Lae. In so doing, Parer and his new company pilot, New Zealander Charlie Pratt, made the first crossings of the towering Owen Stanley Range, which bisects the eastern third of the island. After sneaking between the jagged peaks at 12,000 feet, the two aircraft became trapped above a blanket of cloud and were forced to head out over the Solomon Sea in order to descend. Over the water they let down through cloud so turbulent that Pratt, concentrating desperately on keeping control of the Bristol, was unable to operate the hand pump that kept pressure in the fuel system. Fortunately, he was carrying a passenger who, despite being desperately airsick, managed to lean forward into the pilot's cockpit and pump the tank, keeping the engine running.

The two aircraft broke out of the clouds at 1,000 feet and eventually landed at Lae. The Bristol lasted only three months before it was wrecked in a landing at Wau. But the D.H.9C seemed to ensure Parer's financial success. With it he was able to carry on his air service, which increasingly concentrated on lifting passengers from Port Moresby across the Owen Stanleys to Lae. It was a dangerous flight along a route notorious for black rain squalls, thick clouds and strong winds, with nothing below but jungle, where a crash meant almost certain death. Parer succeeded in these pioneer flights and made enough money to purchase a second D.H.9C.

But his by-now legendary bad luck struck again. As Parer told the story, he had somehow persuaded Sir Hubert Murray, the Lieutenant Governor of a section of New Guinea called Papua, to go for a spin in his brand-new plane. Sober, impassive Sir Hubert was accompanied by his niece, a Miss Morrison. After strapping them into the passenger seats behind the cockpit, Parer revved up the engine and roared down the runway. The plane was barely airborne when the engine quit. Parer had no choice but to plow into the trees at the end of the airstrip, peeling off both wings and smashing the nose. Concerned about his passengers, he jumped down and ran back to Miss Morrison. She stumbled out speechless and disheveled. Sir Hubert, almost a caricature of British upper-class imperturbability, stared at Parer through a pair of flight goggles.

"Excuse me, sir," said Parer, "don't you think you ought to get out?"

"Is it all over?" asked the Lieutenant Governor.

"We've had a crash," said Parer.

"Oh," replied Sir Hubert, "I thought it was one of your stunts."

The aircraft was a total write-off, but Parer continued to fly his older D.H.9C (his D.H.4 was so dilapidated by this time that it was no longer safe to fly). Nevertheless he earned enough to buy a Fokker F.III single-

Ray Parer's modified Bristol Fighter pokes from a primitive hangar at the palm-thatched headquarters of his Bulolo Goldfields Aeroplane Service.

A pilot and his passenger sit side by side in the cockpit of a Junkers W 34 transport, introduced to New Guinea by Pard Mustar's Guinea Airways in April 1928. With a 420-hp engine, the W 34 surpassed any other plane then flying on the island: It cruised at 100 mph and took off, reported Mustar after a test flight, "like a shot out of a gun."

engined monoplane. It was Parer's first bona fide transport aircraft and it was similar in capacity to the Junkers W 34s being flown by Guinea Airways. He seemed prepared at last to give Pard Mustar's outfit some stiff competition. Parer proudly bought some comfortable cane chairs that could be placed in the Fokker's enclosed cabin when the plane was carrying passengers as well as cargo.

On March 18, 1931, he took off from Salamaua on one of the new Fokker's first flights. Parer had two passengers aboard—one of them a woman, the other a man prospecting for gold—plus considerable cargo. Once again it was a case of Parer's Luck as his engine died at the critical point of lift-off. The Fokker careered into the trees, flipping onto its back. Neither Parer nor his male passenger was hurt, and the woman escaped with nothing worse than a fractured wrist; however, the new Fokker was a total wreck.

This crash wiped out Parer financially, but the gold miners rallied to his support. The Battler had given them so many free flights when they were down and out that they now passed the hat for him, raising enough money to buy a replacement aircraft, a Fokker F.VIIA capable of carrying eight passengers. With the Fokker, Parer launched a new bush-flying service he called Pacific Aerial Transport, or PAT.

To ensure that his enterprise succeeded, Parer rarely refused a cargo, no matter how unusual. On one occasion, he spent most of a morning cramming a cow aboard PAT's new Fokker. The unusual consignment was to provide the gold miners with the luxury of fresh milk. Parer took off from Lae only to have the beast jab a horn through the plywood partition that separated the cabin from the pilot's compartment. The enraged animal kept goring until a horn penetrated the back of Parer's seat. The cow then proceeded to give the alarmed airman a series of insistent jabs that persuaded him to race the Fokker at full throttle all the way to Wau.

On another occasion he allowed a friend to bring a wild boar on board. Its legs seemed firmly tied, but the animal nevertheless broke loose at altitude and threatened to destroy the Fokker as it squealed and grunted and smashed about. Fortunately, the boar's feet soon plunged through the floorboards of the cabin, where they stuck fast, immobilizing the animal until Parer reached his destination.

For emergency landings, Parer established an unusual procedure that depended principally on a large bottle of beer. The beer was not intended as refreshment, but to probe potential landing spots. When faced with the unexpected need to land, Parer would make a low pass over a likely-looking patch of ground and, leaning out of the cockpit, drop a bottle of beer over the side. If the bottle burst, spewing its white foam, Parer judged the surface firm enough for a landing. If the bottle survived the impact, the ground was obviously marshy and Parer would search for another site.

Battling Parer's unorthodox methods and casual attitude toward aircraft maintenance—it was said he would fly any plane as long as the propeller turned—contributed to his numerous crashes, but by some miracle he avoided death or even serious injury. Other pilots flying in New Guinea were not as lucky. One victim of the island's peculiarly difficult combination of razor-backed mountains, shrouding mists and sudden blinding tropical storms was a veteran Australian airman named Les Trist.

Trist was working in 1931 for Guinea Airways, flying the company's Junkers W 34s from Lae into the Bulolo gold fields. On May 22 he took off on what promised to be a routine flight—and simply vanished. Virtually all the pilots in New Guinea quickly joined in a search for Trist's plane, sweeping back and forth over the mountains and valleys of the Lae-Salamaua-Wau triangle and then beyond, hoping to spot wreckage in the jungle—and also to spot Trist patiently sitting next to it awaiting rescue. The Junkers had carried plenty of food, water and first-aid supplies, and Trist was skillful enough to have crash-landed without killing himself. Ground parties of men with experience in New Guinea's jungles waited for the lost Junkers to be sighted from the air so that they could walk in to the rescue.

But days of intensive aerial search produced nothing. Not a scrap of the Junkers' silvery metal skin could be discovered. It was as if Trist had flown off the face of the earth.

One day almost three months later, a pilot who had recently arrived in New Guinea, Ian Grabowsky, was mowing the grass along the edge of the Lae airdrome. He had been hired by Guinea Airways to replace Les Trist, but a series of minor accidents involving the company's planes had left him temporarily without an aircraft to fly. As he mowed, Grabowsky looked up to see a group of tribesmen approaching him out of the rain forest. They wore little besides fur arm bands and necklaces of cowrie shells, with a few spectacular bird of paradise tail feathers in their hair. One of the tribesmen carried a string bag, and they all seemed to speak at once in a language Grabowsky could not comprehend, pointing at the bag, at their own heads and then at the airstrip. Stopping in front of Grabowsky, the man with the bag suddenly upended it, and out tumbled a human head. It had belonged to Les Trist.

The bushmen had not murdered the pilot; they had happened across the wreckage of his plane near the crest of Wampit Gap, 25 miles inland. When a ground party later arrived at the site, it became clear why the craft had escaped discovery. The plane and what was left of Trist were scattered across a jungled hillside in so many bits and pieces that there was nothing to salvage or to bury. It appeared evident that Trist had broken a fundamental rule of bush piloting—"no see, no fly." He had plunged into one of the towering cloud banks that appear abruptly on the edge of the range almost every day, thinking that he could make it blind through Wampit Gap. Instead Trist had slammed into the side of a mountain. He had paid the ultimate price for a moment's folly.

A few months before Les Trist's crash, Guinea Airways had increased its lead over the competition when it purchased a Junkers G 31 trimotor, the largest plane yet flown in New Guinea. Junkers had designed the G 31 as a passenger carrier for Lufthansa, but with the seats removed the plane proved an excellent freight hauler *(pages 110-115)*.

A short time later two more of the planes were brought to New Guinea. These belonged to Bulolo Gold Dredging Ltd., which had arranged for Guinea Airways to fly and maintain them. The mining company needed the big G 31s to airlift huge dredges into the gold fields. Surface gold was fast disappearing, but mining engineers working for this international consortium had determined that the gravel and mud in the Bulolo riverbed contained rich gold deposits down to a depth of a dozen or more feet. Company engineers designed special dredges that could be airlifted from the coast to the Bulolo River in pieces and assembled there. The largest air-freighting operation yet seen anywhere on earth was about to begin.

Pard Mustar, who had retired briefly to Australia after years of hard flying and bouts of malaria, returned to Lae to oversee the airlift. Under his guidance the Guinea Airways pilots, flying their own outfit's Junkers G 31 as well as the two owned by Bulolo Gold—they had been christened *Peter* and *Paul* and were augmented two years later by a third named *Pat*—commenced a shuttle service between Lae and the digs, using a new and better airfield that had been built on a flat area at Bulolo, a few miles from Wau.

Most pieces of Dredge No. 1 (eventually eight were built) easily fell within the capacity of the G 31, but two crucial parts weighed nearly 7,000 pounds each. They were the dredge's tumbler, which separated gold from worthless rock, and the shaft on which it turned. The two flights necessary to airlift these components to Bulolo were

The wingless fuselage of a Junkers W 34 stands on its nose after the plane smashed into the jungle short of the airfield at Wau. To the sorrow of prospectors from nearby gold fields, the craft had been carrying a load of bottled beer for the local pub.

Ray Parer's Lady Lettie (left) safely touches down near a Guinea Airways Junkers G 31 trimotor parked on the treacherous incline of the Wau airstrip. At far right, porters wait to unload Parer's cargo.

undertaken by Ian Grabowsky and another experienced bush pilot, named Alan Cross, in November 1931. They waited for fine weather, then filled *Peter's* and *Paul's* tanks with only an hour's fuel to keep the planes as light as possible. Cross and Grabowsky managed to get their heavily laden planes off the runway at Lae and completed the 40-mile flight over the mountains and down into the Bulolo Valley without incident.

When the dredge commenced operation on March 21, 1932, there were speeches, cheers and innumerable toasts—and mountains of good food and liquor imported from Australia for the occasion. In 1931-1932, Guinea Airways pilots had carried a staggering 3,947 tons of freight. By contrast, all the airlines in the United States lifted only 513 tons of freight in 1931, those of Great Britain 649 tons and those of France 1,508 tons.

Although front-running Guinea Airways had captured the lion's share of the heavy-freight business, Ray Parer and a mixed bag of small operators were still able to earn a living flying lighter loads in an assortment of smaller aircaft. One such pilot was RAF-trained Bill Wiltshire. He generally preferred to go it alone, but like most bush pilots

in New Guinea, he also flew on occasion for Ray Parer and Guinea Airways. Wiltshire was a nonconformist with a handlebar mustache whose preferred method of spending his off-duty hours was to meet the steamers from Australia when they stopped for a day or two in Salamaua to unload. Exchanging his grubby flying clothes for immaculate whites, Wiltshire would ensconce himself in the ship's bar, hoping to strike up a shipboard romance with one of the female passengers. If he was unable to find a romantically inclined companion, he would drown his sorrows—disposing of the empty beer glasses by feeding the tops into the blades of the ceiling fan, then tossing the bases out a porthole.

Despite his bibulous off-hours, Wiltshire was unsurpassed as a pilot. On one occasion he saved one of Guinea Airways' Junkers trimotors during a trial flight after the plane had undergone an overhaul at Lae. Wiltshire noticed during preliminary ground tests that the aircraft vibrated ominously. But the mechanics were unable to locate any problem, so the pilot taxied out for a test hop. He pushed the throttles forward, and the unladen plane vaulted into the air after a short takeoff run. The aircraft had barely left the ground, however, when a blade flew off the center propeller. In an instant the resulting lopsidedness twisted the engine and its mount from the nose of the aircraft. The engine bounced down the airstrip, and to the horror of those looking on, the now-unbalanced plane pitched up almost vertically. A crash seemed unavoidable.

Superb pilot that he was, Wiltshire instantly pulled back all the throttles and rammed the big control wheel forward to keep the plane from stalling and plunging to earth. Only a few seconds had passed, and Wiltshire found himself still above the runway. He made a near-perfect landing and brought the aircraft to a halt a few yards short of the end of the strip.

Wiltshire also survived one of Bulolo's more spectacular crashes. Flying in from Lae in a small de Havilland Moth, he encountered the strong crosswinds that often spring up in the afternoons in the Bulolo Valley. Crosswinds persisted over the airfield, forcing Wiltshire to make a slow, cautious approach. Just as he was about to land, a freak downdraft smashed the little plane into the ground. The undercarriage flew off, the propeller was smashed and the lower wings crumpled. Then the Moth bounced up into the air and crashed back down once more, this time on its back. Unbelievably, the pilot walked away only slightly injured.

Undaunted, Wiltshire continued to fly into the gold fields. One day he did the impossible, making nine trips to Wau flying a Guinea Airways Junkers W 34, only to beat this record by completing 10 flights on another day. During most of his runs, and against all regulations, he carried a pet dog in the cockpit, a mongrel of uncertain ancestry that he simply called Pooch.

The gold finds had focused world attention on New Guinea, and

At Lake Kutubu in the central highlands of New Guinea, tribespeople prepare to unload supplies from a Guinea Airways seaplane. The transport was an aerial life line to the isolated Lake Kutubu police camp, established by Australia in 1937 to explore and patrol the uncharted region.

in the 1930s several expeditions arrived to explore the huge, 1,500-mile-long island's hitherto-unknown interior. Anthropologists were fascinated by the opportunity to study cultures that remained in the Stone Age. Interest sharpened when two Australian prospectors, Mick Leahy and Mick Dwyer, became lost while seeking new gold fields as rich as those at Bulolo and wandered deep into the interior. There, cradled in the highlands of eastern New Guinea, they discovered vast grasslands inhabited by an unknown people. Bush pilots quickly became involved in the dangerous business of flying explorers and prospectors into the interior, or of flying out those wounded during encounters with New Guineans, who frequently resented the white man's intrusions.

Ian Grabowsky was among the first bush pilots to fly explorers deep into central New Guinea. He discovered that the people who lived there were often struck with awe by his airplane, falling to their knees and bowing their heads toward the huge birdlike machine. And Grabowsky was not above intensifying their awe, in the interest of keeping his skin whole. On one flight to resupply an expedition waiting for him on a rocky terrace 500 feet above a river, he witnessed what he estimated to be 1,000 warriors clustered nearby. After bringing his de Havilland Fox Moth to a stop, Grabowsky climbed out of the cockpit dressed in a manner guaranteed to inspire the bushmen's respect. "He was wearing a white flying suit," one member of the expedition recalled, "and a white helmet, with large square-cut green goggles. Even to us he looked a bit like an artist's conception of the Man from Mars." The tribesmen gathered about simply flattened themselves on the ground and moaned, afraid even to look upon this gleaming apparition from the skies.

By the mid-1930s the gold fields had become the preserve of the big companies. The eight giant dredges were in operation—every part flown in by the island's bush pilots, who year after year established new world freight records. Guinea Airways had taken over several smaller companies, including Ray Parer's Pacific Aerial Transport. Parer himself, not caring to work for others, was again running a one-man service. The restless adventurer had opened a new gold mine on the Sepik River, 300 miles west of the Bulolo, and was shuttling in supplies. The official aviator's guide, *Notices to Airmen,* stated that there was no chance of making a forced landing in the desolate Sepik country, yet somehow he survived 17 such landings in the bush—and true to his nickname, Battling Parer managed each time to repair his plane and fly out.

Other independent bush pilots continued to operate, carrying geologists searching for oil, flying for Lutheran and Roman Catholic missions that had been established throughout the island and ferrying in teams of scientists intent on studying New Guinea's unique people, flora and fauna. They also carried the small freight items that planes had been taking into the gold fields from the start—medicines, tools, batteries and whiskey—as well as more dangerous cargoes such as blasting detonators and the explosive gelignite.

Following Japan's attack on Pearl Harbor in December 1941, New Guinea's bush pilots found themselves playing a new role. When Japanese aircraft began bombing the island and invasion seemed imminent, the aviators made use of every available plane to help ferry hundreds of women and children to Port Moresby, where they could then board ships for Australia. From towns, villages, mines and missions, with complete disregard for themselves, the bush pilots carried the refugees to safety.

One remarkable flight was accomplished by Norman Wilde, a veteran miner who was also a pilot. At Port Moresby, Wilde came across an abandoned de Havilland Moth, which normally carried a pilot and one passenger. "I didn't know what condition the engine was in but I filled her up with petrol and hoped for the best," he remarked later. "In that Moth I took 11 Chinese from Salamaua to Port Moresby in one hop." To Wilde it seemed as though it had taken him at least a mile and a half to get off the ground and then he "scraped some treetops near the 'drome.'"

Wilde then made a second mercy flight, carrying a group of women and children from Wau to Port Moresby. Japanese fighters and bombers were roaming the skies, but Wilde successfully eluded them, flying to safety by ducking through clouds and skirting mountain peaks.

A Catholic missionary pilot, Father John Glover, and an engineer named Karl Nagy managed one of the great rescue flights of that desperate time. First they threaded their way through the ridges of the highlands to take medicines and supplies to 77 refugees and sick soldiers who were being cared for by a nurse in an isolated mountain village. On their return flight they hoped to reach Thursday Island at the northern tip of Australia. But they came down, out of fuel, on the southwest coast of New Guinea and were paddled partway across the Torres Strait in a native dugout before a passing vessel picked them up. Father Glover then convinced Australian authorities that the stranded soldiers and refugees could be rescued. Several days later, Father Glover, who had been given the temporary rank of captain, returned with two unarmed Qantas D.H.86 biplane airliners and evaded Japanese fighters to rescue all 77 men and the brave nurse from the village. The gallant priest was killed after the War while attempting a landing on one of New Guinea's airstrips, his aircraft caught in a violent downdraft.

The Japanese had taken Rabaul on New Britain and were expected to invade Lae any day when the last bush pilots ferried their few remaining aircraft to Australia. Most of the others had been destroyed already by Japanese air attacks, including the faithful Junkers G 31s. By ones and twos the surviving bush aircraft of New Guinea headed south across the Torres Strait—old single-engined Junkers, beat-up de Havilland biplanes and even a tiny trainer that somehow managed to beach-hop its way 1,500 miles. This ragtag assortment of planes proved valuable to the Royal Australian Air Force, which was critically short of aircraft for noncombat duties. Many of the bush pilots were soon fighting in the skies over Europe and the Pacific.

The two great pioneers of New Guinea aviation, Pard Mustar and Battling Parer, were both too old to fight a second war in the air. Parer was accepted into the RAAF, but detested flying a desk, so he resigned and took a job as engineer on a small coastal steamer. Sailing under orders of the U.S. Navy, Parer's ship carried out clandestine operations along the Japanese-held northern coast of New Guinea. Though nearing 50 years of age, he was still a rugged customer, as he proved the night a Japanese soldier scrambled on deck when the ship was at anchor in a sheltered inlet. Parer killed the knife-wielding enemy in hand-to-hand combat. On another occasion, he rowed ashore and went duck shooting on the Japanese-occupied coast.

Parer survived such adventures, as he had the years of flying in New Guinea, and died of natural causes in 1967. His great rival, Pard Mustar, died four years later, also one of the handful of New Guinea's bush pilots to die in bed.

Aviation in New Guinea thrived again after the War. Three large Australian airlines, Qantas, Trans-Australia and Ansett, established regular service between the major towns, but small bush outfits soon reappeared, ranging into the depths of the country to bring the white man and his strange cargoes to tribes still isolated from the 20th Century by all but impassable mountains and jungle.

The tribesmen's introduction to the white man's *Balus,* or "bird," was sometimes traumatic, sometimes humorous. In the 1950s pilot Peter Manser, flying a Taylorcraft Auster J-5, was carrying a young man of the Dreikikir tribe home from a farm where he had been working. The passenger, who had never flown in a plane, sat nervously alongside the pilot, clutching his ax and a red wooden box of trade goods. Suddenly the engine stopped and Manser, realizing they were going to crash, reached past his petrified passenger and opened the door. In a pidgin dialect he yelled, "As we hit the treetops, jump out of the plane quickly."

Moments later they stalled onto the dense jungle canopy. The young man bailed out still clutching his precious possessions. Thick vegetation broke his fall, and he came to rest on the ground, bruised but not seriously injured, 100 yards from the crashed Auster and the unconscious pilot. Somewhat angered by the whole business, he gathered his possessions and strode off toward his village.

Manser recovered from the crash and was present some time later when his erstwhile passenger was questioned about the crash by government investigators. They had great difficulty keeping straight faces when the young man, in pidgin, told them that he would be happy to fly again in the white fellow's "big *Balus,*" but wished they could provide a better way of getting off. 〜〜

A ceremonial airplane headdress reflects the vivid impression that bush pilots and their flying machines created among New Guinea's inhabitants. The aircraft's three propellers and the windows drawn along its fuselage suggest that the headgear was modeled after a Ford or Junkers trimotor.

Rugged giant of the jungle

In 1930, at the behest of Guinea Airways and Bulolo Gold Dredging Ltd., the Junkers aircraft company in Germany converted a handful of its roomy G 31 airliners into the only cargo carriers in the world capable of flying heavy dredge parts into New Guinea's interior. By the standards of the day, the all-metal airplane was a behemoth, boasting a length of 57 feet and a wingspan of nearly 100. Yet with the help of its outsized flaps and triple-bladed propellers, the Junkers G 31 could take off from and touch down on short airstrips, and it could lug a payload of three and a half tons to 7,900 feet in just 12 minutes.

Such performance ideally suited the craft to the demanding conditions of New Guinea. In April 1931 the planes began ferrying livestock, dismantled dredges and other freight from the coast to the Bulolo gold fields, flying over mountainous jungle that no road had yet penetrated. By the time war put an end to New Guinea mining operations in 1942, G 31s had airlifted 40,259 tons of cargo, and the muscular freighters could claim much of the credit for opening the island's store of gold to exploitation.

A Junkers G 31 cargo plane dwarfs the staff of Guinea Airways at the inauguration of the airline's new hangar and workshop at Lae in 1935. From modest beginnings in 1927, when it operated a single biplane, Guinea Airways grew into the island's busiest carrier, hauling 8,804 tons of freight in 1939 alone.

At the Wau airfield in April 1933, a flatbed truck is hoisted from the cargo space of a G 31. The vehicle, which had been specially designed for the narrow mule track between Wau and an isolated miners' outpost, featured a chassis only three feet wide.

A three-ton boiler is readied for unloading from a G 31. Like other components of the dredge, the boiler was built with the Junkers in mind: It had to be light enough for the plane to carry, and in order to fit through the aircraft's upper cargo hatch, it could not exceed five feet in diameter.

Porters steady a shipment of freight as it is lowered into the cavernous hold of a G 31. The careless loading of heavy machinery could gouge a hole in the plane's soft aluminum skin, and haphazardly positioned cargo could unbalance the aircraft, spelling disaster for the pilot.

A trio of G 31s dominate the Bulolo airfield on March 21, 1932, the opening day of operations for the gold field's first mechanized dredge (top).

A cow is coaxed from a G 31. The transports also ferried in horses for the miners' own race track, the Morobe Turf Club.

4
The lure of Latin America

The cool shadows of the Bar Central in Panama City provided a perfect setting for intrigue and adventure in the sweltering dry season of 1924. In the gloom lurked several Canal Zone characters of dubious appearance—among them a stocky, battered-looking bush pilot nursing a straight Scotch at one end of the bar. His name was Jimmie Angel, and according to him, this was where and when the legend of Devil Mountain was born.

As Angel contemplated his drink, a gnarled old man appeared at his elbow, smacked down a bag of gold nuggets on the bar and ordered the bartender to set up a six-foot row of brandies—perhaps 36 jiggers in all. The old man started belting them down one after another. He announced that he was a prospector, a mining engineer from Denver, Colorado. He had heard, he said, that Jimmie Angel was the kind of flier who would put a man down anywhere there was a clearing large enough to land a plane. No questions asked. There was, the prospector continued, a secret place in the Venezuelan jungles where he wanted to go. The nuggets, worth $5,000, were payment for the flight in and out.

Thus began one of the great tales of bush aviation. Nobody was ever sure exactly how much of Angel's story was fact, and how much fancy. Sometimes the prospector's name was McClintock, sometimes McCracken, sometimes Williamson. But the essential account of the adventure remained the same: a hazardous flight to a "mountain of gold" in Venezuela, a riverbed literally pebbled with precious nuggets—and Angel's lifelong search to rediscover this El Dorado of limitless wealth.

It was a scenario entirely in keeping with Jimmie Angel and the remarkable fraternity of bush pilots, mostly North Americans, who brought air transport to Mexico and to Central and South America in the 1920s and early 1930s. They were genuine heroes, daring pioneers "whose gift of wings," as one historian put it, "enabled them to open new territory for the benefit of mankind." But Angel and his crowd would have laughed outright at the mention of such altruistic motives. Basically, Jimmie and most of the boys were just trying to earn a living. If they could do it by finding gold, so much the better.

Skimming the slopes of Mexico's Sierra Madre, a slow-flying Ford Tri-motor nicknamed La Tortuga—the Turtle—drops toward the runway at Tayoltita, site of the San Luis silver mine.

As Angel told the story of Devil Mountain, he and the aged prospector took off at once from Panama City, flying in Angel's open-cockpit war-surplus Bristol Fighter to Caracas, Venezuela, then to Ciudad Bolivar, 200 miles inland on the Orinoco River. From there they bore generally southeastward, banking this way and that ostensibly for the prospector to search the jungle below for landmarks.

By this time Angel had learned that the old man had covered their route on foot a few months earlier, guided by Indians. The party had scaled a mountain called Auyántepui, or "Devil Mountain," and on its mesa-like top they had found a profusion of gold. The superstitious Indians, fearful of the evil spirits they believed inhabited the remote summit, had then fled, leaving the prospector to find his way down with the few nuggets he could carry. Now he was going back by plane to claim his fortune and airlift it out. It was only a question of finding the mountain and then, of course, landing safely in a tiny clearing near the top. That was why the prospector had chosen Angel.

The mountainous terrain they were flying into, known as La Gran Sabana, was largely unexplored in 1924. Here the lofty trees of the rain-forested Orinoco watershed gave way to tropical highlands tangled with plants and teeming with poisonous snakes. It was sinister country, dominated by a massive plateau that was topped by rain-carved buttes standing like huge totems along the border between Venezuela and British Guiana.

It may have seemed to Jimmie that his passenger had been asking for more maneuvering than necessary to find the way. All the twists and turns were thoroughly confusing; the old geezer was probably lost and would never rediscover his gold strike. But that made little difference to Angel. A northward heading would take them back to the coast and Caracas. He had already been paid for the flight and would come out all right whether they found the mountain or not.

If the pilot's thoughts wandered in these directions, it was understandable—but it was equally mistaken. For as Angel peered through the mists that swirled about these heights, he spotted a mighty butte standing alone above the other jungle-clad hills and rising to a height of 9,000 feet. The old prospector excitedly identified it as Devil Mountain. Angel climbed through the turbulent gusts that whistled around the mountain until the Bristol cleared its summit. The crest was bare of trees but was strewn with boulders and spires of rock. To land a plane there was inconceivable. But just below the crest Angel saw a clearing sandwiched between a swift-flowing stream and a sheer cliff.

Using all the skills accumulated in his years of bush flying, Angel neatly sideslipped the Bristol into the clearing. Before the plane had even rolled to a stop, the prospector was climbing out and running for the stream. For three days Angel helped the old man pan for gold and pour the heaps of nuggets into gunny sacks.

Near the end of the third day, long before the sacks were full, Angel heard thunder booming. His passenger yelled for him to get back to the plane. A huge tropical storm was approaching with ominous speed, and if they did not take off at once, the Bristol might be blown off the top of Auyántepui, leaving the two men stranded.

Angel said later that he ignored usual takeoff procedures and simply launched the Bristol over the cliff, relying on a 3,000-foot drop—a vertical runway in effect—to accelerate the plane to flying speed. When the two men reached civilization, the prospector tipped Jimmie for his services with a few extra nuggets and went home to Denver, promising to get in touch when he wished to return to the stream for more gold.

The narrator of this remarkable tale was born James Crawford Angel in Springfield, Missouri, in 1899. He was fond of telling people that he had blundered into aviation when he was 14 by volunteering to stand in for a circus performer in a balloon stunt, after the man had broken his leg. The balloon was filled with hot air, and little Jimmie—wearing red tights and a green sash—soared aloft. He was supposed to parachute to earth over the crowd but instead he clung desperately to the balloon. He was wafted 40 miles by the wind and came down atop a chicken coop some hours later when the air inside the balloon cooled.

Jimmie's father welcomed him home with a sound thrashing and a promise of more to come. But the young aeronaut evaded further punishment by returning home the next day with a fistful of circus earnings. Waving the cash under his father's nose, he demanded, "How much money did you make today, Pa? I made 75 bucks!"

In 1916 Angel enlisted with other war-eager lads in Britain's Royal Flying Corps. Trained in Canada and then England, he was soon piloting a Farnborough F.E.2b pusher biplane over Belgium. The youngster knocked down three German aircraft before he was shot down himself. Ironically, Jimmie was ferrying an unarmed Nieuport 7 toward the front when his number came up. Jumped by German fighters behind Allied lines, he could neither evade the enemy planes nor defend himself—his plane for some reason carried no machine guns and soon succumbed to a hail of German bullets. Jimmie escaped the ensuing crash with little more than scratches.

It was at this time that Angel began to show a natural gravitation toward exotic places. Hearing that Lawrence of Arabia was in need of pilots, he wangled an assignment to Alexandria, Egypt, and was soon shooting up Turks in the desert. Later he got himself attached to the Italian air force as a test pilot for a new Caproni bomber. That assignment took him to Jerusalem on a demonstration flight. From there he returned to North Africa, where he finished the War helping to establish an air route between Cairo and Cape Town for the RFC.

After the Armistice, Angel bounced around from cockpit to cockpit. He flew in China, joined the U.S. Army Air Corps, resigned and became a test pilot in Chile before heading north to Mexico. There, he had a taste of bush flying—odd jobs carrying mine payrolls and occasionally some mail. At last he had found his calling, the rough-and-tumble life of the bush pilot south of the border, and soon he was running a one-plane air service in Panama, where he met McCracken, McClintock, Williamson—or whatever the prospector's name really was.

Expecting his money to do better for him in the United States, Angel took his service to California, where he sank most of the $5,000 he had been paid for flying the old man to Devil Mountain into materials for a plane he planned to build himself. Through the 1920s he performed all manner of flying jobs. He worked as a test pilot for the California aircraft manufacturer Claude Ryan. He flew a Gotha bomber in Howard Hughes's film *Hell's Angels* and did some stunt flying in William Wellman's *Wings.* But then the Depression struck. It seems that Angel might have attempted to replenish his funds by rediscovering the bonanza on Devil Mountain. But he insisted that he never even tried. Perhaps he felt that the gold rightfully belonged to the man who had discovered it. Whatever the reason, Jimmie Angel, broke and on the move again, headed back to Mexico, resisting the urge to travel farther south to Venezuela and Auyántepui. In Mexico he managed to get hold of three airworthy craft and resumed the mail and payroll flights of 10 years earlier. This time, however, he had solid contracts with the Mexican government and with mining companies. The money may not have been rolling in, but Jimmie was doing all right for himself.

Then in 1931 the old prospector telegraphed Angel that he was dying and asked the pilot to come see him. "The mountain's all yours now," he said when Angel arrived in Denver, but the stricken man was unable to describe precisely the landmarks that had led him there, and it had been seven years since Angel had flown the zigzag course. Even if he could retrace the route he might not recognize the mountain. For all he knew, the clearing near its summit had long ago been claimed by jungle. It was all well and good to "inherit" the gold, but finding it was another matter. Nevertheless, Jimmie decided to make a try—and the search consumed him to the end of his days.

To be nearer his goal, Angel decided to move his bush operation south to Venezuela and traveled to New York to arrange for financial backing. There he met a mining engineer named Durand Hall of the Case Pomeroy Company, a California firm that was testing gravel beds in the Paragua River region of Venezuela to see if they contained enough gold and diamonds to merit a major investment in dredging.

Angel quickly convinced Hall of his flying prowess and was offered the job of company pilot in Venezuela. In his spare time, he would have opportunities to go off on his own in search of the lost mountain.

Accompanied to Venezuela by Hall, Angel met the field representative of the firm, L. R. Dennison, and the three became fast friends. The two engineers were amused by the aviator's fantastic yarns, but they could see that he was a first-class pilot, and that was what counted. When he raved about mysterious mountains and lost gold, they just laughed it off.

Hall and Dennison built an airstrip at Paviche, southeast of Ciudad

Bolivar on the Orinoco River, and Angel began flying the company Cessna out of the jungle field in 1935. One of his official responsibilities was to fly Dennison around a large part of Venezuela to photograph the terrain for a map. The assignment fit right in with Angel's plans, because it allowed him to explore while working. He flew from sunrise to sunset, landing only to refuel and take off again. The two engineers marveled at his stamina and dedication.

Still, Angel occasionally found the time to get himself and his employers in a jam. Late one afternoon he, Dennison and a Case Pomeroy supervisor took off for Ciudad Bolivar and were caught by the abrupt nightfall of the tropics. As Angel sped through the dark, he used the faint outline of the river below to keep him on course toward the city, and Dennison held a flashlight on the instrument panel, which had a short circuit in the lighting system. Angel had landed in the city so often that he knew the location of the field, and as he began his approach, the Cessna's landing lights picked up the reassuring surface of the runway. Then seemingly from nowhere a large herd of cattle loomed in the windshield. Gunning his engine, Angel pulled up just in time. He tried buzzing the field repeatedly to scare the cattle away, but unknown to him, a number of burros were mixed in with the herd. These stubborn animals refused to budge, and the cattle emulated the burros.

In desperation, Angel zoomed over the city center, trying to attract attention before they used up the last of their fuel and crashed. Fortunately a French aviator in town heard the plane and guessed that there was trouble. He raced to the airfield, where he drove the cattle and burros aside.

No sooner had Angel landed than he was arrested by angry policemen. It seemed that he had accidentally buzzed the mansion of the Governor, who was seating guests at an important banquet. Hearing the diving plane and fearing that they might be under attack by revolutionaries, the formally garbed ladies and white-tied gentlemen hit the floor in heaps. Jimmie apologized for the disturbance, but the Governor would not be placated until Angel and Dennison had spent three days in the local jail as punishment.

Whenever crazy adventures and routine company flights did not interfere, Angel continued his search for Devil Mountain. He had come to realize that the erratic course of the original flight had been the prospector's deliberate deception to protect his find. There was a chance that they really had landed on the peak called Auyántepui, but it was just as likely that the old man had called it Devil Mountain to confuse Angel.

During one of his innumerable scouting trips across La Gran Sabana, Angel made a discovery that assured him at least a small measure of lasting fame. Flying past the shoulder of a massive mountain, Angel suddenly saw magnificent white tendrils of water spilling over the edge of a butte and plummeting vertically like long strands of silken hair into the jungle below. Flying downward from the top of this stupendous waterfall, Angel estimated with the help of the plane's altimeter that it was more than 3,000 feet from top to bottom. Jimmie could hardly believe his eyes. In all his travels, he had never seen—or even heard of—anything that compared with it.

Angel was silent about his discovery. His stories about the riches of Devil Mountain had brought him only ridicule. He was not going to invite more of the same with tales of this extraordinary cataract. But he was unable to keep the news from Hall and Dennison. As expected, they laughed. However, one fine day, the two scoffers agreed to go up with Angel for a look at his "wonder."

The men were obviously indulging their pilot, but the smirks faded as Angel banked around a mountain and the cascading waterfall came suddenly into view, just as Angel had described.

"God!" was all that Hall could say.

"Unbelievable," Dennison mumbled.

"I guess I've lost my title to world champion liar," said Angel.

Some time later, when a team of explorers from the American Museum of Natural History penetrated the Venezuelan jungle and measured the waterfall they found it to be the highest in the world; at 3,212 feet it was 20 times taller than Niagara. Named Angel Fall in the pilot's honor, the cataract made Angel world-famous for a time. But it did not distract him from his search for gold.

Not even love and marriage could distract him from his quest for long. In 1934 he had met a stunning 26-year-old redheaded secretary named Marie Sanders at the home of mutual friends in Los Angeles. For Marie, it was love at first sight. "After listening to him for 15 minutes," she later recalled, "I was hooked." So was Jimmie. Within two hours—and in front of their friends—he blurted out his proposal. After little more than a moment's hesitation she stammered, "Yes," then thought to herself, "God help me."

Angel had to leave California on business the next day, but returned the following year to claim his bride. Soon they were married and on their way to Venezuela so the pilot could continue his search for the old prospector's legacy. There Marie was immediately initiated into a life of adventure. Jimmie deposited her at an abandoned Indian village in the wilderness some 160 miles southeast of Ciudad Bolivar, said the place was to be their home and the very next day flew off on an errand, leaving her with only a pistol for company. Minutes after he departed curious Indians armed with bows and blowguns appeared and gathered outside a hut where Marie had taken refuge. Terrified, she crouched inside trembling, and remained there for a day and a long, sleepless night. By the time Angel returned on the afternoon of the second day, the Indians had drifted away and Marie had resolved that the only way to cope with her new life was to swallow her fear. When Jimmie asked if she had been afraid, she replied calmly: "Afraid? Afraid of what?"

Besides a wife, Angel by now had acquired a new plane, a seven-passenger Flamingo with an extra fuel tank to increase the aircraft's range; just how he financed the purchase was never quite clear. In

In a picture taken late in life, Jimmie Angel's puffy, battered face serves as a reminder of his many scrapes with death as a bush pilot in Latin America. Most of the scarring came from a fire that broke out in a Ford Tri-motor he was piloting over the Andes.

The tallest cataract in the world, Angel Fall cascades 3,212 feet down the cliffs of Auyántepui Mountain in eastern Venezuela. Discovered by Angel in 1935, the falls are fed by a fantastic 300 inches of rain a year and emerge from the mouth of a great subterranean river carved through the rock by centuries of erosion.

1937, he decided that if he concentrated his search during the dry season he would come upon the bare patch on Devil Mountain where he had landed with the prospector. After some months of flying over La Gran Sabana, Angel at last spotted a clearing on a butte not far from Angel Fall and next to a stream.

The pilot was elated. He flew home and a day or two later returned to the site with Venezuelan explorer Gustavo Heny, a friend named Miguel Angel Delgado and Marie, who had insisted on joining the expedition at the last minute. Angel swooped down among the rock spires, dropped the Flamingo onto a secure-looking bald patch—and then was horrified to feel the plane's wheels sink beneath the surface of what was really a bog. The Flamingo flipped onto its nose. No one was hurt, but clearly this was not the spot where he had landed before. No gold was to be found. Chagrined, Angel led the others down the mountain on foot. With little food or water, the party suffered an agonizing 14-day journey around perilous crags and down steep bluffs. The Flamingo remained where it crashed.

It is probably safe to say that never in his entire life had Jimmie Angel felt more frustrated. He had found no gold and his plane was an unsalvageable wreck. He had been through enough to discourage any man, and shortly after this episode, he and Marie left Venezuela. During the next 19 years, Angel continued to live and work pretty much as he always had, flying for fun and profit. In time, he and Marie settled outside San Jose, California, to raise their family, a pair of sons.

An improvised nose hangar fashioned from a bed sheet provides some protection from the weather for Angel's Ryan monoplane during engine repairs at Camarata, his base camp near the foot of Venezuela's Auyántepui Mountain.

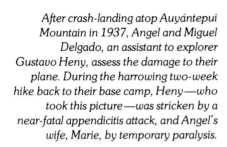

After crash-landing atop Auyántepui Mountain in 1937, Angel and Miguel Delgado, an assistant to explorer Gustavo Heny, assess the damage to their plane. During the harrowing two-week hike back to their base camp, Heny—who took this picture—was stricken by a near-fatal appendicitis attack, and Angel's wife, Marie, by temporary paralysis.

From all appearances, Jimmie had abandoned once and for all the search for the elusive bonanza of Devil Mountain. But hopes die hard, and old adventurers get restless. In 1956, when he was pushing 60, Angel headed south for one last attempt to find the gold-laden stream. But while taxiing his Cessna 180 on a runway in Panama, a freak cross-wind flipped the plane over. Jimmie suffered a cerebral hemorrhage and died in a hospital. In keeping with his will, his ashes were strewn over Angel Fall, deep in La Gran Sabana. "Of course it was no dream," Marie protested years later when the subject of Devil Mountain came up. "Jimmie wouldn't have risked our lives for nothing."

Jimmie Angel's opposite in many ways was a New Zealand-born pilot named Lowell Yerex, a sober, hardheaded aviator who pioneered more air routes in the Southern Hemisphere than anyone else. Gold did not fuel his ambition; a pure love of flying and adventure did.

Like Jimmie Angel, Yerex was a veteran of service in France with the Royal Flying Corps. Shot down over enemy territory in 1918, he escaped from a German prison train by waiting until the guards fell asleep and then jumping through an open window. After the War, Yerex went to the United States and for five years barnstormed around the country in his own Standard biplane. After giving up that precarious way of life for a brief and unsuccessful stint selling Hudson automobiles in Santa Fe, New Mexico, Yerex drifted south of the border and back to aviation.

He landed in Mexico, flying for one of that nation's first air services. It was an outfit founded by an American adventurer named Theodore T. Hull and called Corporación Aeronáutica de Transportes, or C.A.T. In 1929 Hull bought a fleet of the finest small planes of the era, including several seven-passenger Lockheed Vegas, and inaugurated the first trans-Mexican air route, a 638-mile flight from Matamoros to Mazatlán on the Pacific Ocean. Soon Yerex and C.A.T.'s other pilots were flying their planes on another route, still longer and more taxing, that connected Mexico City with distant Juarez, just across the U.S.-Mexican border from El Paso, Texas.

These flights over the largely barren Sierra Madre were fraught with peril. Two of Yerex's fellow pilots and their passengers died in crashes against mountainsides, victims of the freaky weather that left the peaks almost always shrouded in mist.

As for the airfields, a C.A.T. pilot named Gordon Barry recalled years afterward the dangers posed by the short airstrip at Juarez, which was on a mesa 200 feet above the surrounding desert. Trying to take off on one occasion, Barry realized he would not make it and locked the brakes. "Still she skidded 300 feet," Barry recalled, "turned over, skidded some more and finally ended with the tail of the plane in the air and almost hanging over the edge of the cliff—in thin air."

C.A.T. also contracted to fly supplies into isolated mining camps in the mountains, which was even more perilous work. Yerex was among the first pilots to take a plane to the San Luis silver mine, landing on a short strip that had been hacked out of the side of a mountain. The winds that whistled through the canyons imposed a restriction on C.A.T. operations. Gordon Barry noted that it was best to fly into and then out of the San Luis mine's airstrip early in the morning, before the sun-heated canyon walls created severe turbulence.

Hull's C.A.T. air service went broke in 1932, a victim of the Great Depression. Its main routes were taken over by an already expanding Pan American World Airways. But by that time Lowell Yerex had struck out on his own. In 1931, foot-loose, jobless and with only $25 in his pocket, he came across a pair of Americans in Mexico City who owned a four-place Stinson Junior biplane. They were a prospector named Henshaw and a former air charter operator named Pounds, and they needed a pilot if they were to turn a profit with the plane. Their proposal was simple: For a salary of $100 a week Yerex would fly them in their Stinson to Honduras, where there was little government regulation of aviation. Once there, he would make the plane pay by flying charters, taking up joy riders and hauling freight between Honduras' isolated towns.

During the first month, Yerex grossed an astonishing $3,600 for his employers, who passed the time in Tegucigalpa's cool bars while their energetic pilot ferried people and freight from one cow pasture to another in stifling heat. At this time, much of Central America lacked railways or even one-lane dirt roads. Honduras was in effect two countries, with lofty mountains separating the ports on the Caribbean coast from the capital, Tegucigalpa, on the Pacific side. The choice for a traveler wishing to get from one to the other, as a historian of Central American aviation has put it, "was not between public land vehicles and airplanes, but rather between eight days by burro and 30 minutes by air."

In such a situation, a pilot with the zeal and tenacity of Lowell Yerex could hardly fail to turn a profit. He grabbed business from the few other pilots then offering air charter service in Honduras by undercutting their rates. The standard price of a flight across the mountains from San Pedro, a principal city in the northwest, to Tegucigalpa was $55; Yerex charged $40. He also flew national and local politicians about Honduras on campaign junkets, and in so doing made powerful friends.

Yerex's efforts paid off handsomely for the owners of the Stinson, but not for Yerex himself. Henshaw and Pounds drank up the profits and failed to set aside Yerex's wages. After weeks of such slavery, Yerex flew the Stinson to La Ceiba on the northern coast of Honduras. Having placed 120 mountainous miles between himself and the plane's bibulous owners in Tegucigalpa, he informed them by telephone that, in lieu of back pay, he would accept half ownership of the aircraft. It is not clear what Yerex intended to do next if his stratagem failed, but it did not, and Yerex became part owner of the Stinson and the charter service he had labored to build. By year's end he had bought out his partners, and early in 1932 christened his burgeoning bush-flying service TACA, an acronym for Transportes Aéreos Centro-Americanos that would soon become famous throughout the region. By the end of the year Yerex had turned his $25 grubstake into a business worth perhaps $30,000.

But it was politics, not business acumen, that propelled Lowell Yerex out of obscurity into phenomenal success. In 1929 there had been an election in Honduras that resulted in a peaceful transition from a conservative government to a liberal one—the first time in the 110-year history of the nation that a regime had relinquished power without violence. In 1932, the year Yerex founded TACA, Honduras tried to repeat the performance. Again, voters turned out the government, but this time supporters of the ousted regime launched an armed uprising.

The president-elect, Tiburcio Carías Andino, immediately hired Yerex to fly reconnaissance sorties over the rebel strongholds. Some authorities on the history of Central American bush flying claim that Yerex's contribution to President Carías' cause went beyond mere aerial reconnaissance and included bombing raids on rebel positions. The bombs were said to have consisted of large milk cans filled with nuts, bolts and other bits of metal packed around sticks of dynamite.

Though relatively safe in the air, Yerex did not emerge from the revolution unscathed. While making a routine reconnaissance flight, he and his mechanic prepared to set down on the grassy airstrip at Cerro de Hule, a mountain town only 10 miles from Tegucigalpa that was supposed to be firmly in the hands of troops from the capital. Yerex banked his Stinson into a steep approach to the minuscule strip, sideslipped to lose altitude and then bumped down on the crude airfield. The plane had hardly rolled to a stop when, to Yerex's dismay, an armed insurgent emerged from the surrounding underbrush and began firing a small-caliber pistol. A bullet smashed into Yerex's face, injuring one eye. The mechanic flying with him rushed forward from the rear of the plane to help and found the pilot dazed, the cockpit splattered with blood. But Yerex collected his wits, turned the Stinson around, took off and flew back to his Tegucigalpa base. Somehow he managed to land, but surgeons could not save his eye, and a short time later Yerex traveled to New Orleans to be fitted with a glass eye.

While he was in a hospital there, the rebellion in Honduras petered out, and Yerex returned to a hero's welcome. President Carías was so grateful for Yerex's contributions to the success of his cause that he offered a cash reward, which Yerex shrewdly declined in favor of certain special privileges and perquisites. The most important was a contract from the Honduran government to fly the mail. This contract, which amounted to a government subsidy, put TACA on a firm financial footing. Yerex also received the right to import new aircraft, spare parts and other materials needed to run his air service without paying Honduran customs duties.

Yerex continued to fly despite his loss of an eye, compensating for the resulting lack of depth perception with his now-considerable experience in slipping planes into small jungle and mountain airstrips. As TACA continued to grow, it undertook its first flights outside the country—to neighboring El Salvador and then to Nicaragua, Costa Rica and Panama—and Yerex acquired a number of additional planes, including a handsome high-winged Bellanca monoplane.

Despite its expansion into something resembling a proper airline, TACA remained essentially a bush-flying operation. Yerex and his men had to build their own airstrips without government assistance, often bargaining for use of the land with promises of free flights for the owner and his family. Then Yerex would recruit local labor to remove trees, underbrush and large rocks. A nucleus of this labor team would be retained to chase cattle off the field whenever a plane was due to land.

Many of these primitive strips were cleared near the Caribbean or Pacific coasts of the Central American countries TACA served. But a number of TACA's stops were in the mountainous interiors, where level ground was almost nonexistent. "It was not unusual for the strips to terminate at the face of a mountainside or at the edge of a ravine," according to one historian. "Sometimes a plane would be out of sight when it landed, until it literally taxied up the hill and over the crest of the runway before reaching the air terminal." These mountain strips, if short and dangerous, were usually dry. Many of the coastal fields, however, had poor drainage. During the rainy season, TACA's pilots were forced to learn the location of soft, swampy spots on the so-called runways or risk digging in a wheel and nosing over.

By 134, Yerex owned the first of several Ford Tri-motors. All of them, in the best bush-flying tradition, had been acquired secondhand by the economical Yerex. For each of the Fords, then being phased out by airlines in the United States, Yerex paid $3,000 to $4,000. When new, they had cost $50,000 apiece.

Yerex flew the Fords under astounding conditions. The airstrips that he and his pilots took off from were theoretically both too short and too bumpy for such a heavy aircraft. But the sturdy planes rarely balked at the rough treatment. In an early test of his Tri-motors, Yerex filled one of

Little more than a speck against the Mexican Sierra Madre, a mining company transport climbs steeply after taking off from Tayoltita in the 1930s.

At the Tayoltita airstrip in northern Mexico, a lone passenger sits on his luggage as government soldiers guard a stack of gold and silver bars awaiting shipment by Corporación Aeronáutica de Transportes. The wooden steps at left were used to board the company's aircraft.

the planes with heavy machinery, food and other supplies, and set out to deliver the cargoes to the Agua Fria mine, right in the center of Honduras' most rugged mountain area.

Flying from the port of San Lorenzo on the Pacific side of Honduras, the Ford was forced to climb to 6,000 feet to get over a nearby spur of mountains and then thread its way through passes to reach the mine, which was at 3,300 feet. Yerex flew in a 50-ton flotation-and-cyanide mill, used in refining the ore, a 450-horsepower hydroelectric plant and two compressors, each 320 feet long. Such heavy machinery was, of course, disassembled in San Lorenzo for air shipment and flown to the mine in pieces. But some of them were so large that they would not fit through the plane's door. So TACA mechanics cut a four-by-six-foot hatch in the Ford's metal skin, right over the door, and loaded the plane with the aid of a hoist. To equip the mine fully, TACA Tri-motors were flying what amounted to a shuttle service with as many as 24 flights per day into the mountains.

Yerex and his air service provided a similar life line for another mining company, this one in Nicaragua. The La Luz gold mine also was up in the mountains, 50 miles from the nearest port. In six years, TACA ferried 30,000 tons of equipment to the mine, mostly in Fords. One Tri-motor was fitted with a huge 600-gallon tank that took up so much space in the fuselage that the pilot had to climb into the plane through the top of the cabin. The tank was filled with diesel oil at the port of Alimicamba, then emptied at the mine site. In one day, this long-suffering aircraft could deliver 2,400 gallons of the fuel needed to keep the mine operating.

Yerex's freight operations were not restricted to transporting needed gear to mines. TACA also did a thriving business in hauling valuable or perishable goods out of the remote jungle and mountain areas of Central America. Coffee, fruit, beans and tobacco were all carried by the

Local townspeople gather around the C.A.T. Bellanca Air Bus at the Tayoltita airstrip in 1931. The Bellanca, used to ferry in fresh food, mail, passengers and spare parts, was a profitable bush plane, since it could carry nearly twice as much as the line's standard Lockheed Vega.

Ford Tri-motors and other aircraft, as were mahogany timber and the pliant gray sap of the chicle tree, the essential ingredient in chewing gum. By 1938 TACA had grown to 30 aircraft and was carrying eight million pounds of freight a year, along with some 20,000 passengers.

But hard times were ahead for Yerex and TACA. The problem was giant Pan American. If TACA had continued merely to operate within Central America, Pan Am's chief, the formidable Juan Trippe, might have looked the other way. But when Yerex merged TACA with American Export Lines, a U.S. shipping company, Trippe began to fear that Yerex might be granted air routes to the United States, making TACA a direct rival to Pan Am throughout Latin America. Trippe began legal maneuvers to block the deal on the ground that it was against United States law for a surface carrier to own an airline. In Guatemala—a hub for Latin air routes—Pan Am suddenly sponsored a new national airline, and the Guatemalan dictator abruptly canceled all TACA's rights in that country. Yerex lost his mail contract and his Guatemalan airstrips were expropriated. The new Guatemalan airline received the latest aircraft from Pan Am's fleet.

Realizing that these developments would spell the end of TACA, Yerex sold the controlling interest in his airline to a group of United States investors. One of them was billionaire Howard Hughes, already the major stockholder in another airline, Transcontinental and Western

Air. Hughes planned to link Yerex's routes with Transcontinental's, but he never succeeded in doing so. By 1951 nearly all TACA holdings in Central America were liquidated, and the company's one remaining base there was in El Salvador.

The sale of TACA stock made Lowell Yerex wealthy, and after World War II he moved to Argentina. There he took up an entirely new line of work—building railroads for the regime of dictator Juan Peron. Yerex added to his millions, but unfortunately he could not get his money out of the country; by Argentine law his assets were frozen within the nation's borders. Yerex lived modestly in Argentina, his chief pleasure being a membership in the Hurlingham Country Club, a bastion of Englishmen and Scots who had immigrated to Argentina to build, like Yerex, the country's railways, streetcar lines and other major engineering works. Yerex died of cancer in Buenos Aires in 1968 at the age of 72.

He will be remembered, however, not for his railroad construction, but for TACA, which he built into the most extensive bush-flying operation in history. It epitomized the pioneering spirit of the airmen who opened up otherwise inaccessible places on the globe.

Shortly after Lowell Yerex left Mexico in the early 1930s to form TACA, his place was taken on some of the gold-mine runs by a supercharged Mexican youth named Leo Lopez. For the next 50 years Lopez would continue to fly, becoming one of the legendary bush pilots for his skill, his unflagging energy—and his longevity.

Lopez was born in 1909 in El Paso, Texas, where his parents had fled to escape the roving *bandidos* who were then terrorizing northwestern Mexico. Entranced by aviation, the young Lopez had barely finished high school when he volunteered to sweep hangar floors and clean the airplanes at the El Paso airport. For a time he was paid nothing, then he was given a less-than-munificent $2.50 a week. The situation took a turn for the better, however, when two flight instructors at the El Paso field volunteered to give the bright-eyed, hard-working youth free flying lessons. By 1929, when Lopez was only 20, he was already barnstorming the Southwest and dodging antiaircraft fire as he flew photoreconnaissance missions for the Mexican government against encampments of rebels around Juarez. From then on Lopez seldom spent a day without flying on a payroll delivery, a mercy mission or an exploration of the territory he staked out as his own—the vast Mexican state of Chihuahua.

Lopez began flying from Chihuahua City, the capital, in 1931 as an instructor for the Mexican Army's fledgling air service. He was soon helping Yerex's old sidekick Gordon Barry fly supplies and payrolls into the mining camps nestled among the Sierra Madre, or flying gold and silver bullion out. Lopez' first plane was an antique Jenny, but he eventually acquired a Ryan monoplane that was a near duplicate of the one Charles Lindbergh had flown across the Atlantic. The Ryan was unsatisfactory at first. Its original 300-horsepower engine was not powerful

This picture of Leo Lopez was taken in 1934, three years before he bought a Ryan Brougham monoplane, shown at right above undergoing field maintenance somewhere in Chihuahua, Mexico. Shortly after acquiring the aircraft, he replaced its engine with a more powerful one, purchased for $350 from the U.S. Army Air Corps airplane graveyard in Tucson, Arizona.

enough to take the plane into the Mexican mountain country. Lopez, with a bush pilot's flair for improvisation, simply grafted a much larger and heavier 420-horsepower Wright engine onto the plane's nose. He doubled the size of its ailerons for better control at high altitudes, where the air was thinner, and added wide balloon tires to cushion landings on crude strips. With this mongrel aircraft, Lopez could lift a half-ton load.

Often he carried gold or silver, but a more dangerous cargo consisted of glass containers of highly corrosive muriatic acid, a chemical used to refine the precious metals from ore. This was frightening work. Any crash that broke the vessels, spilling acid on the pilot, promised a horrid death. Such a mishap could occur on landing or takeoff—or at the hands of bandits, who tried to shoot down the gold- and silver-laden craft. Lopez devised special techniques for avoiding these thieves and making safe landings in the Sierra Madre. "You must take a zigzag pattern," he once told a pilot he was training, "and not a straight route. You must be careful you do not fly over an area where there is no place to land. Always know where the riverbeds are and the treeless areas."

On his charter flights into the gold mines, Lopez sometimes flew eight, 10 and even 12 hours a day, often returning to his home base after dark. Since the field at Chihuahua had no runway lights and Lopez' planes also lacked landing lights, he smoothed the field with a layer of sand, which he covered with white lime. A layer of salt on top kept the lime from fading and provided a luminous strip that stood out at night under the illumination of stars or moon.

For a brief time in the mid-1930s Lopez varied his work by flying for a small bush airline, Communicaciones Aereas Veracruz, that specialized in taking payrolls into oil drilling areas near Tampico on the coast. "Bandits massacred the people trying to take the money in on muleback," he recalled. He then received a reserve commission in the Mexican Army and became the service's top flight instructor.

133

With all this behind him, Lopez was still only 32 years old in 1941 when he founded Servicio Aereo Leo Lopez, acquiring a second Ryan monoplane, a Ford Tri-motor, a Stinson Detroiter and a Piper Cub. Airlifting supplies and personnel into mining camps continued to earn the bread and butter, but Lopez soon became better known for the many, usually unpaid, mercy missions he made as his way of thanking Providence for preserving him through so many dangerous flights.

In 1935, for example, when a student uprising in Villahermosa, southeast of Mexico City, was ruthlessly put down by the Governor, dozens of students were left dead or dying on the city's streets. Lopez immediately took off in the Tri-motor, although he knew that he, too, might be caught in the shooting. After flying 300 miles through rain, clouds and strong winds, he landed at the Villahermosa strip at dusk and made his way into town with his copilot and radio operator.

They checked into a small hotel for the night, locked themselves in and "didn't venture out 'til morning," said Lopez. "We weren't shot at, but there was still an unsettled feeling about."

Next day, about a dozen of the most severely wounded were carried to the airport on stretchers by their families. Lopez and his crew had a local doctor bandage the students to stem the bleeding, strapped them into the Tri-motor's seats and took off for Mexico City, where the best medical facilities were. The trip was so bumpy and the students so weak, recalled Lopez, that "they kept dropping over on each other." Only four survived.

With all these activities, Lopez also applied himself to establishing a radio communications network in Chihuahua. The idea germinated in the winter of 1939, when Lopez was trapped far from home by foul weather. His wife, Aurora, fearing he had crashed, was frantic with anxiety. On his return, Lopez and his wife took a brief course in radio mechanics and built a small set he could carry in his plane. Thus equipped, he could send a radio message when he was delayed that would be forwarded to his wife. Unfortunately, few Chihuahuans had radios that would pick up his signals. So Lopez set out to persuade the people of outlying *estancias* and communities to acquire their own radio transmitters and to have the government assign them call letters. He argued that such a network, aside from letting him contact Aurora, would enable people to call for aid in emergencies. Before long, nearly 500 tiny radio stations were licensed in Chihuahua, and Lopez, having set up what amounted to a one-man Mexican version of Australia's Royal Flying Doctor Service, answered many distress calls himself, frequently without pay.

Once he picked up a miner who had been severely burned and flew him to a hospital. Some months later a man wearing dark glasses presented himself at Lopez' house. "Your husband Leo saved my life up at the mine," he announced when Aurora opened the door. He wore the glasses to hide scars left by the accident. "I've come to pay him partially," he continued. "I have only 400 pesos,

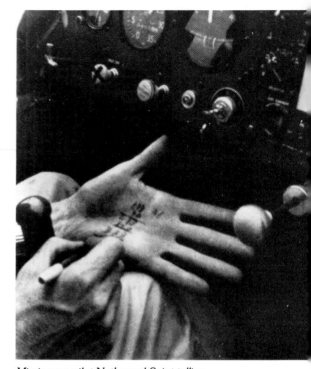

Missionary pilot Nathanael Saint tallies up the weight of cargo aboard his plane on the palm of his hand. In the hot, thin air of the Ecuadorian jungle, each pound added another foot or so to the length of the aircraft's takeoff run.

but I'm going back to work and will send more as I make it."

"Don't leave any money," Aurora said. "He has already been paid."

"Who paid him?" the man wanted to know. "I'll pay that guy back."

"The Lord paid him, and that's all my husband needs," she replied.

Whether it was divine protection or simple flying skill that allowed him to fly for so many years over Mexico's rugged cordillera, Lopez continued to run Servicio Aereo Leo Lopez into the 1980s and still gave lessons at a flying school he had established. He has been honored for his contribution to Mexican aviation—and the quality of life in his adopted Chihuahua—with several international awards, including recognition by the Fédération Aéronautique Internationale, the organization in Paris that encourages progress in aerial navigation and safety and keeps track of records set by planes and pilots. The Fédération gave Lopez its highest award for "distinguished aviation achievements."

After World War II an entirely new sort of bush pilot emerged in the Americas, the flying missionary. If the airplane could open hitherto inaccessible regions of the world to commerce, it could also, missionary groups perceived, help bring Christianity and the benefits of modern medicine to the tribes that lived in the rain forests of Central and South America.

As a rule, missionaries were not pilots; they needed skilled aviators to fly them to the tribes they sought to help. Seeing the need for such a flying service, James Truxton, a Navy pilot, joined other military aviators and in 1944 organized such an outfit based in Los Angeles. Combat pilots during the War, they were eager to spread the doctrines of the Bible as soon as peace was restored. After the War, they were joined by a remarkable young man named Nathanael Saint whose mission it became to adapt the airplane in surprising and original ways to the support of missionaries operating in that wildest of all the world's bush areas, the upper reaches of the Amazon.

Nate Saint was born in 1923 in Huntingdon Valley, near Philadelphia, Pennsylvania, the seventh child in a family of pious Christians. His luxuriantly bearded father designed stained-glass windows, including the famous Rose Window at the Washington Cathedral in the nation's capital. His mother, a Wellesley graduate, was the daughter of an inventor. Young Nate combined his grandfather's zest for mechanical things—especially machines that flew—with his father's lifelong devotion to religious works.

Saint joined the U.S. Army Air Forces during World War II. He hoped to fly, but a childhood attack of the bone disease osteomyelitis dashed any chance of pilot training. He had to be content with becoming a mechanic and a crew chief.

Saint was still in the Army in 1945 when he discovered his vocation in a clipping from *The Sunday School Times* that described Truxton's newly organized bush-flying service. The idea fascinated Saint and fired him anew with the ambition to fly. As soon as he was discharged, he

An aerial view of the Auca village shows a communal hut that could hold 50 people, and three sheds next to a stream. These structures and others nearby served the village's population of about 300 Indians.

A missionary holds Saint's canvas bucket as the pilot passes overhead. Saint found that by lowering a field telephone in the bucket, he could speak to someone on the ground for minutes on end.

Standing beside his yellow Piper Family Cruiser, Saint displays an Indian headdress, which had come up in his bucket, and a kettle festooned with ribbons that he planned to lower to the Auca.

Portraits of the missionaries with presents from the Indians identified the men to the Auca as the source of airborne gifts.

Flying missionaries bearing gifts

As a college student, missionary pilot Nate Saint had noticed that a pencil tied to one end of a long string remained stationary as he moved the other end in a circle. Applying the same principle years later to bush flying in Ecuador, he found that while circling in his plane, he could lower a canvas bucket on the end of a 1,500-foot line right into the arms of someone standing on the ground.

The "bucket drop," as Saint called it, proved crucial in efforts to establish arm's-length contact with Ecuador's fierce Auca Indians before meeting them on the ground. Saint's first overture was a metal cooking pot, delivered late in 1955. When it became clear that the Indians had accepted this offering, other gifts—machetes, a chicken, clothes and buttons—soon followed. All told, Saint made 13 weekly drops. On the sixth one, the Auca responded by sending up a feathered crown; on another, they offered a tame parrot in a basket. The give and take encouraged Saint to think that the Indians might be friendly after all.

The Auca's parrot perches near its basket.

bought a used Piper Cub and became a pilot at last, earning both private pilot's and instructor's tickets at a flying school near his Pennsylvania home. Thus qualified, he soon joined Truxton's flying service, which would come to be called the Missionary Aviation Fellowship, or MAF.

Saint's first assignment was in southern Mexico, where a team of linguists was at work in the jungle near the Guatemalan border. They wanted to translate the Bible into the local Indian language, which they first had to decipher. Keeping the team supplied with food and medicines by pack train was an ordeal, so MAF's Elizabeth Greene, a former member of the Women's Airforce Service Pilots, provided air support with a four-place Waco biplane. Saint was needed in Mexico to keep the aircraft flying.

After several months of this backup work, Saint was offered the choice of two assignments: flying for MAF in Ecuador, where missionaries had made great strides among the Indians, or going to New Guinea, where there was a major effort under way to convert the people of the interior valleys. Saint chose Ecuador, largely because it seemed the greater challenge. Ecuador's rain forests on the eastern slopes of the Andes were primeval wilderness. Here, along the tributaries of the upper Amazon, dwelt two tribes not yet reached by missionaries, at least not by any who lived to tell about it. One was that of the ferocious Jivaro head-hunters, who used blowguns with poison-tipped darts to kill their enemies. Their neighbors were the equally bloodthirsty Auca, whose standard greeting for strangers was a needle-sharp hardwood spear.

His choice made, Saint returned to the United States in 1948 and married Marjorie Farris, a nurse he had met while visiting in Los Angeles. Soon afterward, he was flying a Stinson Voyager to Ecuador, accompanied by Marjorie and by Jim Truxton. In October, Saint and his bride arrived at Shell Mera, a Shell Oil Company outpost on the eastern slope of the Andes and near the edge of Auca country.

The Shell exploration crews were willing to share the fine airstrip at Shell Mera. Saint set to work immediately, flying daily rounds to far-flung missionary stations. His new wife manned the radio at Shell Mera to maintain contact with isolated missionary families and listen for distress calls from aircraft.

Shortly after arriving in Ecuador, Saint had a crackup; his plane was smashed to earth by a violent downdraft just after takeoff. His worst injury was a fractured vertebra that put him in a body cast. While recuperating, Saint turned out the first of several inventions—an emergency fuel system for high-wing monoplanes in case the main fuel line clogged, interrupting the flow of gasoline to the engine. In the Amazon jungles, where there were few places to land, a choked-off fuel supply meant almost certain disaster. Saint's invention consisted of two cooking-oil tins mounted beneath the wing, with a fairing whittled of balsawood for streamlining. A copper tube, containing a valve that could be opened from the cockpit, carried the spare fuel from the tins down a strut to the engine. The system worked flawlessly, and Saint

Squatting beside Saint and a model of his yellow Piper Family Cruiser, an Auca Indian whom the missionaries nicknamed George munches a hamburger while Roger Youderian, another member of Saint's party, daubs him with insect repellent. Saint later presented the model to George.

later patented the idea after it was approved by the U.S. Civil Aeronautics Administration.

Saint had become an experienced jungle pilot when, near the end of 1955, the time came at last to approach the dreaded Auca. Operation *Auca* was not Saint's idea or especially his mission, but as the local MAF pilot he figured heavily in carrying out the dangerous encounter.

The plan was to locate the nearest Indian settlement and attempt to befriend the inhabitants first with gifts and later with kind words. No outsider had successfully approached the Auca in many years; those who had tried had been ambushed and slaughtered. But Saint had a way to make first contact safely from 1,500 feet in the air. It was a means he devised of lowering objects to earth by rope from a flying plane, and he called it the "bucket drop" *(pages 136-137)*.

Scouting flights over Auca territory soon established the site of a settlement near the Curaray River not far from Shell Mera. Each time Saint flew over the huts in the yellow Piper Family Cruiser that had become his regular plane, he saw signs of habitation, but no Auca were visible. To lure them out, Saint and a companion, Ed McCully, lowered a large aluminum cooking pot and left it in a clearing. "In a sense," Saint wrote in his log that night, "we had delivered the first gospel message by sign language." On the second airdrop—this time the gift was a bright new machete—Saint and McCully saw immediately that the aluminum kettle was gone. They also saw, to their intense excitement, three Auca emerge from a large leaf-covered house. "They were already watching their dangling prize," Saint recalled, and when the machete accidentally splashed into the river, an Auca instantly dove in to retrieve it. Thirteen more drops followed, one a week, through November and into December of 1955. Besides items of hardware, the missionaries also sent down clothing—T-shirts, dungarees and a checkered shirt that was appropriated by the Auca leader.

In late December the missionaries decided that the time had come to make contact on the ground, face to face. By way of introduction, Saint first dropped photographs of himself, Ed McCully and the three other missionaries who had organized Operation *Auca:* Peter Fleming, James Elliot and Roger Youderian. Saint then surveyed the jungle near the Auca settlement, searching for a spot to land. A sand bar on a nearby branch of the Curaray seemed to offer the best chance of a safe landing.

On January 2, 1956, Saint circled and came in for the first landing. The sand was soft, but Saint hugged the stick to his belly and prayed; the plane did not flip. He and McCully jumped out quickly and removed any rocks and sticks that looked threatening. Then leaving McCully behind to spend the night, Saint took off low over the river and headed for home. It seemed quite possible to set up a base on the sand bar, which the men dubbed Palm Beach.

Jim Elliot and Roger Youderian accompanied the first load of supplies, which included a walkie-talkie for communicating with the plane, food and other basic equipment. On the next trip Saint took in a radio powerful enough to contact Shell Mera directly and building materials for a tree house, where the missionaries would be relatively safe should the Auca stage a surprise attack. Two more flights and the base was established. On January 5, Peter Fleming joined the other four men. They were excited, but watchful. "It is no small thing," Saint wrote that night, "to bridge between the 20th Century and the Stone Age."

On the morning of Friday, January 6, three Auca suddenly stepped out of the jungle across the river: a girl, an older woman and a young man. Though Saint had seen Auca wearing clothes that had been sent down to them, these Indians were naked, and they seemed friendly.

Jim Elliot waded the 20 yards to the opposite bank of the stream and led the unresisting trio across to Palm Beach. The male Auca was about 20 and showed no sign of fear. The three Indians chattered happily among themselves and stayed all afternoon. When the warrior, whom the missionaries nicknamed George, showed an interest in the Piper, Saint decided to take him up. George was so entranced with his first flight that he insisted on a second ride, shouting delightedly all the way. At twilight the three Auca vanished into the jungle.

The young missionaries were jubilant. This first meeting with the dreaded Auca seemed a great success. Saturday passed uneventfully, but on Sunday, the missionaries saw a group of about 10 Indians heading for Palm Beach, perhaps attracted by the hymns the young men had been singing. They radioed the news back to Shell Mera, promising

Would-be rescuers examine the remains of Saint's plane (above) after the Auca killed all five missionaries and left their mutilated bodies floating in the Curaray River. Saint, acutely aware of the danger inherent in his work, had nevertheless insisted that "missionaries who know the joy of leading a stranger to Christ gladly count themselves expendable."

further bulletins as soon as they had something to report. But then their radio fell silent.

Alarmed by the lack of contact, the backup crew at Shell Mera went into action. One friend flew anxiously over Palm Beach and saw the Piper Family Cruiser slashed to pieces on the sand bar. Nearby lay the body of one of the missionaries. No other bodies were to be seen.

Ecuadorian Army units and a U.S. Air Force helicopter rescue team from Panama were alerted. As a ground party hacked its way through the rain forest toward Palm Beach, the Air Force helicopter rushed ahead, hoping to pluck the rest of the Americans from danger. But it was too late. From the air, the copter crew spotted the bodies of the other four missionaries. They were floating in the water, snagged on branches or aground in shallows. At least one of them appeared to have been beheaded. There was no sign of the Auca.

When the heavily armed ground party arrived, it found that four of the men, including Nate Saint, had been speared. The fifth, Ed McCully, had been hacked to pieces with machetes. Around the shaft of one spear were wrapped the pierced pages of a Bible. The Ecuadorian government sent its regrets to the U.S. Ambassador, but regarded any effort to track and punish the Auca as impractical.

Marjorie Saint went to Quito after the incident to teach. However, the widows of the other dead missionaries insisted that the airdrops of gifts to the Auca be continued by other MAF pilots, so that the Indians might one day be converted to Christianity. In 1957, two Auca women walked out of the jungle into a missionary outpost near Shell Mera and soon befriended Jim Elliot's widow, Betty, and Rachel Saint, Nate's older sister, who had come to Ecuador even before the massacre to study the Auca language. When the Auca women returned to their tribe, the two Americans went with them. They would be safe, the Indians made clear, because they were women. The five male missionaries had been killed, it was explained, because the ever-suspicious tribesmen believed that the white men were cannibals like the Jivaro and had come in their unearthly machine to wipe out the Auca settlement. Fear had led them to do what they later considered a mistake.

Betty Elliot and Rachel Saint stayed among the Auca, treating the dreadful jungle diseases they suffered and translating the Bible for them. "There could be no greater joy," Betty Elliot told friends, "than to know that the blood of our husbands has been the seed of the Auca church."

As for Nate Saint, he left behind, in addition to his spiritual example, valuable contributions to bush flying. His emergency fuel-supply system proved a lifesaver time and again, and his remarkable bucket-drop technique became a boon to aviators flying in the wildernesses of the world. The Missionary Aviation Fellowship expanded after Saint's death from its original handful of pilots and planes into an international organization with autonomous American, British and Australian-New Zealand branches operating in Africa and the southwest Pacific, as well as in South America. ᕕ

Planes that conquered the last frontiers

"The bush planes were pretty machines but they were entirely functional," recalled one flier. "There wasn't a single frill on them. Every piece of equipment had to be useful." The rugged aircraft shown here and on the following pages—with the years they first flew noted in parentheses—have hauled passengers and supplies through every type of weather and over some of the world's wildest terrain.

The earliest bush planes were surplus World War I military biplanes hastily modified for civilian use. But bush flying became a viable commercial proposition only after the appearance of the first closed-cabin monoplanes and the development of reliable air-cooled radial engines during the latter half of the 1920s. The years following World War II saw the production of a new generation of aircraft designed specifically for bush operations.

Since they flew under primitive conditions, even the earliest bush planes had to be easy for their pilots—who were usually excellent mechanics—to maintain and repair. They also had to be versatile craft, and many were equipped with floats or skis. But load-carrying capacity was the most important factor in determining an aircraft's usefulness and profitability. The most successful bush planes of the 1930s could carry half a ton or more of cargo, anything from 55-gallon fuel drums and large pieces of machinery to lengths of pipe. Prudent pilots in addition carried complete survival kits for themselves and their passengers. Even for short flights Alaska glacier pilot Bob Reeve, for example, always kept on board a fire pot with which to thaw his engine, a fire extinguisher, engine and wing covers, a sleeping bag, a 30-30 rifle, an ax and a shovel. He also carried a ration of emergency food and an armful of magazines because, as he explained, "you run out of hamburger and newsstands mighty fast in Alaska."

AVRO 504K (1917)
With a 36-foot wingspan and 100-hp water-cooled engine, the Avro 504K—here in Qantas livery—was the standard trainer of Britain's Royal Flying Corps until the late 1920s. Thousands of the reliable planes were built during and after World War I, and they served bush fliers and the fledgling airlines of a dozen or more countries.

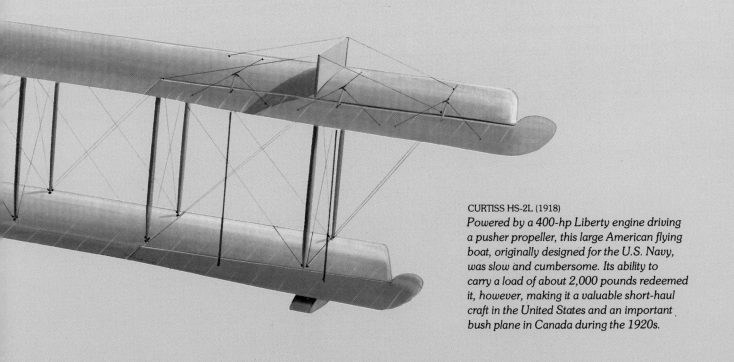

CURTISS HS-2L (1918)
Powered by a 400-hp Liberty engine driving a pusher propeller, this large American flying boat, originally designed for the U.S. Navy, was slow and cumbersome. Its ability to carry a load of about 2,000 pounds redeemed it, however, making it a valuable short-haul craft in the United States and an important bush plane in Canada during the 1920s.

FOKKER UNIVERSAL (1926)
Although it carried four passengers in an enclosed cabin, this early monoplane had an open cockpit for the pilot just behind the engine. The Universal shown here, equipped with a reliable 200-hp Wright Whirlwind engine and fitted with skis and a winter engine cowl, flew for Western Canada Airlines.

JUNKERS W 34 (1927)
A descendant of the famed Junkers F 13, the world's first all-metal transport, the rugged W 34 was produced in both landplane and seaplane versions by its German manufacturer. Powered by a 400-hp radial engine, it was used by airlines in Canada, South America and Africa. This particular aircraft flew for Guinea Airways.

DE HAVILLAND D.H.50A (1924)
A conventional biplane with a 230-hp water-cooled engine, the four-passenger D.H.50A was extremely reliable and saw wide use as a passenger and cargo plane. The one shown here, whose fabric-covered wings and tail surfaces were made waterproof and airtight with colorless dope, was built and flown by West Australian Airways.

BELLANCA CH-300 PACEMAKER (1929)
Developed from the plane in which Clarence Chamberlin crossed the Atlantic two weeks after Lindbergh's historic 1927 flight, the Pacemaker could cruise at 120 mph with normal landing gear and 110 with floats. Its 850-mile range suited it to surveys and long flights over wilderness areas. This craft belonged to Marine Airways of Juneau, Alaska.

STINSON SB-1 DETROITER (1925)
This ski-equipped biplane powered by a 200-hp Wright Whirlwind engine was bought from arctic explorer Captain Hubert Wilkins by Alaska bush pilot Noel Wien for $10,000 in 1927. The plane—with its enclosed cabin, 90-mph cruising speed and 800-mile range—enabled Wien to inaugurate the first year-round service between Fairbanks and Nome.

NOORDUYN NORSEMAN MK. I (1935)
The Norseman was designed for bush flying in northern Canada. Early versions had 420-hp Wright Whirlwinds, but later models were fitted with more powerful Pratt & Whitney engines and became well known as utility planes in World War II. The aircraft shown here flew for Canada's Dominion Skyways.

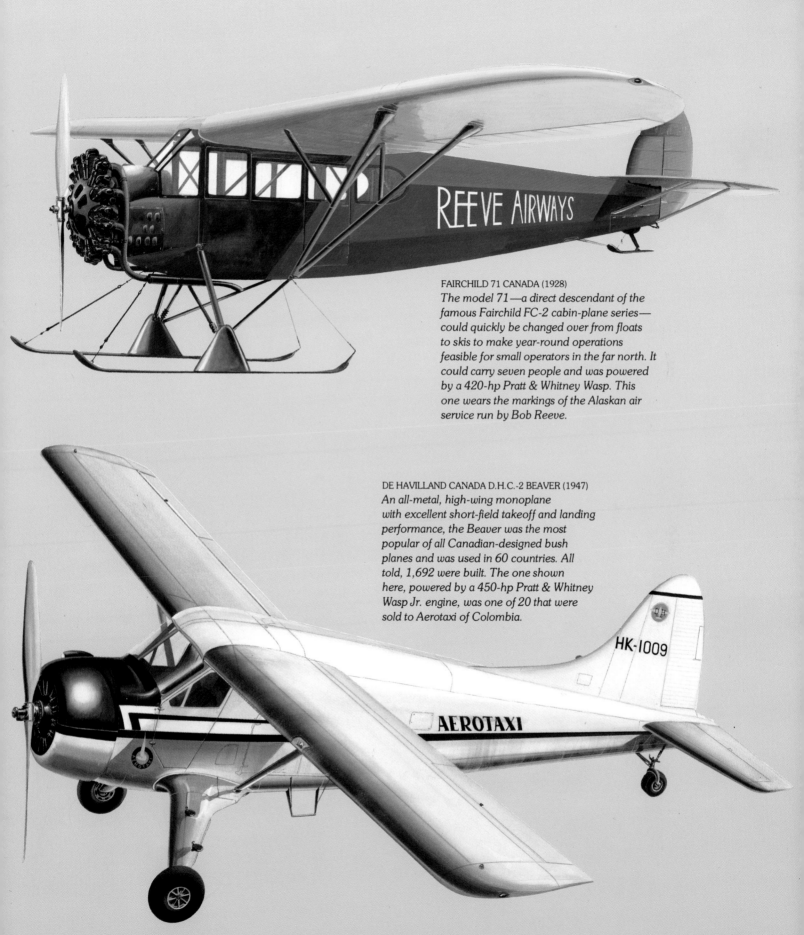

FAIRCHILD 71 CANADA (1928)
The model 71—a direct descendant of the famous Fairchild FC-2 cabin-plane series—could quickly be changed over from floats to skis to make year-round operations feasible for small operators in the far north. It could carry seven people and was powered by a 420-hp Pratt & Whitney Wasp. This one wears the markings of the Alaskan air service run by Bob Reeve.

REEVE AIRWAYS

DE HAVILLAND CANADA D.H.C.-2 BEAVER (1947)
An all-metal, high-wing monoplane with excellent short-field takeoff and landing performance, the Beaver was the most popular of all Canadian-designed bush planes and was used in 60 countries. All told, 1,692 were built. The one shown here, powered by a 450-hp Pratt & Whitney Wasp Jr. engine, was one of 20 that were sold to Aerotaxi of Colombia.

HK-1009

AEROTAXI

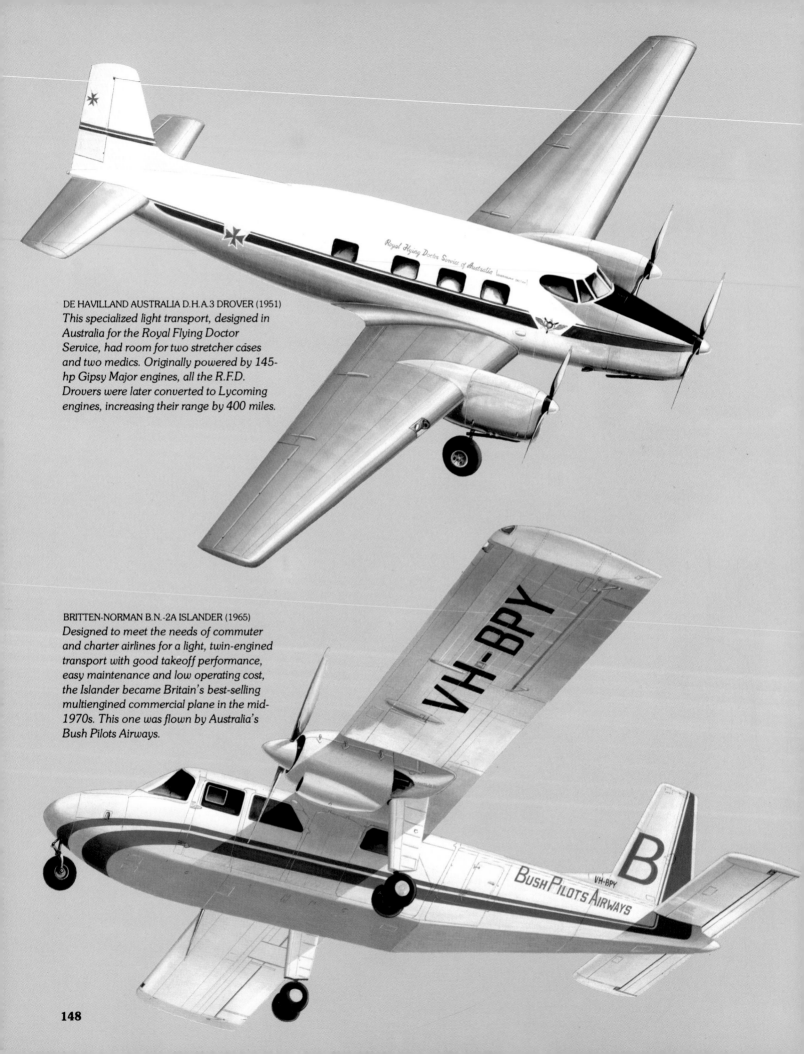

DE HAVILLAND AUSTRALIA D.H.A.3 DROVER (1951)
This specialized light transport, designed in Australia for the Royal Flying Doctor Service, had room for two stretcher cases and two medics. Originally powered by 145-hp Gipsy Major engines, all the R.F.D. Drovers were later converted to Lycoming engines, increasing their range by 400 miles.

BRITTEN-NORMAN B.N.-2A ISLANDER (1965)
Designed to meet the needs of commuter and charter airlines for a light, twin-engined transport with good takeoff performance, easy maintenance and low operating cost, the Islander became Britain's best-selling multiengined commercial plane in the mid-1970s. This one was flown by Australia's Bush Pilots Airways.

DE HAVILLAND CANADA D.H.C.-3 OTTER (1951)
With its 600-hp Pratt & Whitney Wasp engine, this versatile, all-metal utility aircraft could carry up to 14 passengers or a ton of freight. The floatplane version shown here belonged to the Ontario Provincial Air Service and was specially fitted with two 80-gallon water tanks on the pontoons for combating forest fires.

G.A.F. N22B NOMAD (1971)
Developed by Australia's state-owned Government Aircraft Factories, the Nomad is a 12-passenger utility transport powered by two 400-hp Allison turboprop engines. Designed to have excellent handling during short takeoffs and landings, it has been produced in commuter, medical evacuation and military patrol versions. This particular plane was flown by Independent Air Services into interior New Guinea.

A deadly, daily game

Rain, fog and sleet plagued the U.S. Army Air Forces base at Nome during World War II, regularly grounding the bombers and fighters stationed there. And yet even with the ceiling at less than 200 feet and visibility under a quarter of a mile, the men on the ground would often hear the drone of a DC-3's engines as the pilot circled and came in for a landing. At such moments they shook their heads: "Must be crazy," they would say. "Or else it's Jefford." Jack Jefford, an Alaska bush pilot, was the only flier skilled enough to land under such conditions. For Jefford there was nothing unusual in the feat. The Nebraska-born pilot had come north in 1937, settled in Nome and taught himself how to fly blind after installing a gyroscopic compass and an artificial horizon in his plane and covering the cockpit with a hood. "It's like playing a fiddle," he said. "You must practice and practice."

Not surprisingly, when it came time to construct airfields and lay out 8,000 miles of airways in Alaska during the War, the Civil Aeronautics Administration picked Jefford to help get the job done. Jefford, more than any other individual, would thus be responsible for changing the face of Alaskan bush flying forever. No fewer than 30 large airfields, two dozen emergency strips, 56 radio beacons and 66 weather stations were established throughout the wilderness between 1939 and 1945, at a cost to the government of $400 million. At War's end, all these facilities remained, vastly improving Alaskan air communications.

The War brought similar advances to several of the world's other wild areas opened up in the 1920s and 1930s by pioneer bush pilots. In Canada, many airfields were built during the War, and those serving the cities of Canada's huge western provinces of Manitoba, Saskatchewan, Alberta and British Columbia were enlarged and modernized. The exigencies of wartime flying also brought better snow removal equipment to these fields. As a result, heavier aircraft could now fly year-round without skis. Such improvements led to a boom in Canadian postwar aviation, bringing about the disappearance of some small-time bush operations and the evolution of others into scheduled air services.

One bush outfit, Associated Airways Ltd., flying out of Edmonton,

Carrying on the tradition of Alaska's pioneer bush pilots, air charter operator Don Sheldon banks his Piper skiplane over a glacier toward the 20,320-ft. summit of Mount McKinley.

Alberta, grew from two small planes in 1945 to 24 aircraft in 1951. Even more impressive was the growth of Canadian Pacific Airlines, which absorbed at least 10 bush operations in the 1940s and flew a nationwide system of routes ranging from the Yukon in the far northwest to Labrador on the Atlantic. On its larger planes, mostly DC-3s, CPA introduced in-flight meals and further astonished customers, used to roughing it in tiny planes, by employing stewardesses. The provincial governments of Manitoba and Saskatchewan devised their own air services—as Ontario had done back in the mid-1920s with the famous Ontario Provincial Air Service. Bush flying had not vanished from postwar Canada—one-man operations still carried prospectors, now often looking for uranium, into remote lakes and forest clearings—but increasingly the old bush-flying routes were serviced by large planes owned by big companies.

Similar progress had been made in Australia and even in New Guinea, where the U.S. Fifth Air Force, while battling the Japanese, had turned the gold-field strips in and around Lae into modern airfields capable of handling B-25 medium bombers. Yet bush flying remained a difficult and dangerous occupation. Nature was as intractable as ever; a thunderhead could destroy the newest and strongest of planes. Radio beacons were a great aid to navigation, but a pilot still had to know his route by heart. And it still made sense for him to carry every sort of survival gear and maintain his plane with a zeal bordering on fanaticism.

Of the postwar generation of bush pilots, none played the odds more carefully than Don Sheldon. Though many fields had up-to-date fueling systems, he always followed the old practice of filtering his fuel five times through chamois to remove even the smallest droplets of water, which might freeze at high altitudes and cause his engine to misfire. He even filed smooth the tiniest nicks in the edges of his metal propellers to keep the nicks from widening under stress into cracks that could lead to blade failure. Such a development, Sheldon dryly noted, "usually ruins a guy's whole day."

Sheldon's caution did not make him any less of a character. Far from it. Like Jack Jefford, he became a legend in his own time. He routinely pulled off incredible feats of flying that more often than not he dismissed with an "aw shucks" attitude.

A lanky, leathery native of Wyoming, Sheldon had the look, and the twang, of a genuine cowboy. Orphaned at 12, he had started out as a cowboy and frontier adventurer. He had worked on his uncle's small Wyoming ranch for five years, but had never felt entirely at home there. Turning 17, he had struck out for Alaska, lured by the idea of living in America's last great wilderness. Sheldon arrived in Anchorage in 1938, and the only job he could find was in a dairy where he worked, he later said, 25-hour days and nine-day weeks. Whatever he had come to Alaska for, this was not it, so he soon boarded an Alaska Railroad train, determined to ride north as far as his savings would take him—all of 80 miles to Talkeetna, a tiny riverside settlement halfway between Anchorage and Mount McKinley, North America's highest peak.

At first, Talkeetna had even less to offer in the way of a job than Anchorage. Sheldon managed only to make a few dollars chopping firewood. But he soon learned to hunt and fish for food and to trap beaver, lynx and marten for their valuable pelts. In the summer, he found work at a nearby gold mine for 50 cents an hour, 10 hours a day. Occasionally, he would listen as a bush plane roared by overhead. After several months of bashing through the undergrowth on his forays into the wilderness, he came to envy the pilots of those airplanes. "All I could ever think was how much better that kind of travel was in this area of no roads than beating yourself to death on a pair of snowshoes."

Sheldon used some of his savings to enter the University of Alaska in Fairbanks, where he planned to study engineering. When his funds began to run out, he quit. He went back to trapping, but soon landed work with a survey crew, helping build an airport for the Civil Aeronautics Administration at Ruby, and then one at McGrath, at the time the center of Alaskan bush aviation. There he met his first bush pilots, among them Bob Reeve. Reeve "was a rough character and always seemed to be in a heck of a hurry," Sheldon recalled. "Some said that he was actually landing airplanes on glaciers, a feat that I found hard to visualize."

Don Sheldon (left) stands with two trapping friends in front of a beaver pelt stretched out to dry at their campsite on Alaska's Tanana River. Sheldon went on several trapping expeditions during the early 1940s to earn money for his college tuition—and to put something aside for the airplane he hoped someday to buy.

Determined now to fly himself, Sheldon spent some of the money he had earned on the surveying and construction projects to take lessons at a flying school in Anchorage. He received his private license a month after Pearl Harbor and, his heart set on becoming a fighter pilot, joined the U.S. Army Air Corps. To his bitter disappointment, he was trained instead as a B-17 tail gunner and sent to England, where he flew 26 combat missions in B-17s. He also ran a bicycle rental and repair shop on the side, saving enough money to buy a Piper Cub after the War.

The problem, he later recalled, was that when he returned to the States there were no Cubs for him to buy—the Piper Aircraft Corporation at Lockhaven, Pennsylvania, had a backlog of orders. Sheldon would just have to wait for his name to come to the top of the list. Refusing to abandon his dream, he took a job with the company in the hope he might get preferential treatment, and began delivering planes all over North America. After a trip to Mexico, where he dropped off a Cub, he was riding home on a bus when fortune smiled on him in Amarillo, Texas. Through the window he caught sight of an open field full of army-surplus Taylorcraft Cub L2Ms about to be auctioned. He got off at the first stop and two days later bid $1,200 for one of the single-engined observation planes, becoming the proud owner of No. 96.

Sheldon was on his way at last, except for one small detail. The plane had been sitting in the sun and wind so long that its engine was caked with dust and sand. Sheldon had to flush out the carburetor with kerosene before he could take off. When he returned to Pennsylvania, he took another look at the list of back orders. His name was still far from the top. He decided to quit the company and, to celebrate his freedom, pay a flying visit to his sister in Idaho. As he was crossing the Great Divide near Jackson, Wyoming, he was startled by a ripping sound: Thirteen feet of the sun-weakened fabric covering the right wing had peeled off and was caught on his right aileron, restricting its movement. A chance gust could upset the plane and cause it to crash.

Sheldon managed to put down in a field and patch the wing with some burlap bags. The makeshift repairs got him to Riverton, Wyoming, where he replaced the burlap with regular airplane fabric. Then, as planned, he visited his sister. Though he flew all the way back to Pennsylvania without incident, he worried about the airworthiness of his craft and re-covered the entire plane and otherwise refurbished it. To make himself as independent as possible, Sheldon enrolled at the Williamsport Technical Institute to study airframe and engine maintenance. Now virtually self-sufficient, he made up his mind to head straight for Alaska. He reached Fairbanks' Weeks Field in April 1948.

His arrival was well timed. A gale had recently put many of the aircraft parked there out of commission, and Sheldon was hired to help repair them. While at Weeks, he made a return visit to Talkeetna, his prewar home. Friends asked him to start an air charter service. It suddenly struck him that he really could make a living doing something he liked. He moved to Talkeetna in July and shortly thereafter set up the Talkeetna Air Service with a partner called Stub Morrison, so named because his left hand had been lost in an auto accident.

By the early 1950s Morrison was dead, the victim of an air crash, and the modest outfit he and Sheldon had founded had become one of Alaska's premier charter services. Sheldon found himself in a flight schedule that could keep him going from morning until late at night. He flew regularly for the U.S. Geological Survey and the Alaska Road Commission, and took private parties to the Kuskokwim flats in the west, Barrow and Umiat in the far north and Ketchikan and Yakutat on the Panhandle to the south.

In the vast, roadless wilderness that is interior Alaska, Sheldon became, as one writer who flew with him said, "taxi driver, supply line and rescuing angel to an army of trappers, miners, mountain climbers and homesteaders." Along with the passengers in his six-place Cessna 185, he often carried such varied cargo as snowshoes, crampons, cartons of ice cream, dynamite, even cases of eggs. Some of these items he would drop to homesteads or mining camps that had no landing strips, delivering them with unerring accuracy—and, having taken pains to wrap them well, without breakage.

Sheldon loved his adopted Alaska, and no matter how frantic his schedule might be, he would take time to bank and circle when he spotted some interesting sight below, pointing out to those aboard a river roiled by spawning salmon, a cow moose browsing with a newborn calf or scars left on the landscape by an abandoned mining operation. His consuming passion was the great Alaska Range and in particular Mount McKinley with its many glaciers. One passenger recalled how Sheldon, on approaching the mountain, stood his plane on one wing to look down and shout, "This is the Great Gorge of the Ruth Glacier. Deeper than the Grand Canyon, but most people never heard of it."

More than two years of almost daily flying in the Alaskan bush honed a keen edge on Sheldon's skill as a pilot. Yet as good as he was, Sheldon occasionally miscalculated. His first serious accident occurred in the autumn of 1950 on a small mountain lake near Talkeetna. He had flown in with a sourdough friend named Frank Moennikes, to dress and take out two moose that had been shot by hunters. Having loaded the butchered animals aboard the plane, they began their takeoff run. The pontoons were just rising out of the water when Sheldon realized that they were not going to clear a rock escarpment at the end of the lake; the air was still and unseasonably warm, providing insufficient lift. As the obstacle grew larger, Sheldon tried to bear off gently, but the plane stalled, plunged into the lake and sank into the icy depths.

What happened next showed the kind of stuff Sheldon was made of. The impact of the crash hurled Moennikes under the instrument panel, knocked him out and badly sprained his neck, but Sheldon was unhurt and kicked his way out through the broken windshield, dragging the unconscious man behind him. After struggling to the surface, Sheldon swam with Moennikes to a sand bar 100 feet away. Then he returned to the water for a sleeping bag that had popped up from the sunken wreckage. It was bone-dry on the inside, so Sheldon wrapped it around his injured friend and covered it with caribou moss for additional warmth during the coming night.

Sheldon then struck out cross-country for help. He forded swift rivers and forced his way through heavy brush; at one point, he nearly stepped on a sleeping grizzly that crashed away through the undergrowth. Finally, after 14 hours of exhausting struggle, he crested a ridge; below were the tracks of the Alaska Railroad. After vainly trying to flag down a speeding train, he staggered along the railbed until he came upon a shack with railroad workers bunked inside. Using the telephone, they called in a rescue team for Frank Moennikes at the lake. "Sheldon is one good man," said the grateful Moennikes afterward.

It was a narrow escape for all concerned. But misjudgments of any kind were rare for Sheldon. More often, his skill made it possible for him to pull off fantastic feats that would have cost the life of a lesser aviator. In 1955, members of the U.S. Army Search and Rescue Section stationed at Fort Richardson in Anchorage announced their intention to chart the navigable stretches of the Susitna River in a yellow 50-foot boat. This would necessitate their shooting a five-mile stretch of rapids

Don Sheldon strides from one of his Cessna 180s after landing on his home airstrip at Talkeetna, 80 miles north of Anchorage. Though he owned as many as four aircraft at a time, he never insured any, because the annual premiums were too costly—one third the value of the insured plane.

known as Devil's Canyon. Sheldon was amazed that the Army scouts would attempt such a thing. He had flown many times over the canyon, and knew how the water roared between rock walls 50 to 70 yards apart. But the Army team would not be dissuaded, so Sheldon let it be known that he would check on the adventurers from time to time.

The first day he failed to spot the yellow boat on the river. The next day, while flying two fishermen to Otter Lake in a small Aeronca Sedan equipped with floats, Sheldon detoured for a pass over Devil's Canyon and was dismayed to see flecks of yellow in the shadows at the bottom. Quickly, he put his passengers down at Otter Lake and flew back, skimming the rim of the 600-foot-deep canyon to look for the men. "They'd really been clobbered," he later said. "I saw barrels of gasoline bobbing around here and there. The wreckage was strewn downriver to a point almost 25 miles below the canyon, and it consisted mostly of bright yellow chunks of the boat's hull and other debris—but no people."

At last he spotted seven of the men huddling on a spray-washed ledge at the base of the canyon's north wall. They were battered, their clothes torn, their life jackets in shreds. He could imagine them being swept away to their deaths one by one as their strength waned.

Here the canyon was nearly 200 yards across at the top, but down 600 feet, at water level, it was only about 50 yards wide, with the river aboil as the current churned wildly over submerged boulders. Even if he could fly into the canyon and put his pontoons down on the river, he seemed certain to strike a hidden rock—or be swamped by the swirling white water. But something had to be done quickly.

Sheldon spotted a smoother stretch a quarter of a mile upriver, made a couple of practice passes and then landed with his pontoons pointing into the 30-mile-per-hour current. The Aeronca slowed almost at once, but overran the smooth section of river and entered turbulent water upstream. Sheldon advanced the throttle to create a prop wash for the rudder to bite into so that he could keep the pontoons aligned with the current. He began to float backward at 25 miles an hour.

"As the plane backed into the first of the combers," he said afterward, "I felt it lurch heavily fore and aft. It was like a damned roller coaster. The water was rolling up higher than my wing tips, beating at the struts, and I could barely see because of the spray and water on the windows. The engine began to sputter and choke, and I knew it was getting wet down pretty good. If it had quit, I'd have been a goner, but it didn't."

The river became smooth as Sheldon backed over the section he had landed on, then turned rough again. But like some giant water bug, the Aeronca floated lightly on the surface. Suddenly the men on the ledge came into view. Now began the hardest part of the rescue operation. "I had to stop the airplane's backward motion, which I did with full throttle, but I knew my problems had only begun," Sheldon recalled. "Without damaging a wing on the rocks, I had to get the airplane close enough to the ledge for the guys to jump out onto the float and get aboard. If they missed, in their condition, they'd drown for sure. I jockeyed around and

157

finally got the wing angled just enough to get one of them on the left float and still keep myself from running downstream."

With the man aboard, Sheldon let the plane slip away, tail first, for the mile-and-a-half trip to the end of the rapids. "That first trip," he said, "was one of the longest rides on a river that I've ever taken." Clear of white water, Sheldon turned the nose downriver and took off.

It was little short of miraculous that Sheldon was able to rescue even one of the seven men on the ledge—the eighth member of the team had been swept away. Just about any other pilot would have flown home then and there, feeling lucky to be alive. But not Don Sheldon. Now that he had carried out one man, he was convinced that he could go back for the rest, taking out two per trip. This he did, flying into the gorge three times to pick up the stranded men. In a final stroke of luck, Sheldon found the eighth and last man, skinned up and bruised, but without any broken bones, far downriver. In gratitude, the U.S. Army awarded the pilot a special citation. "Seeking neither acclaim nor reward," it read, "Mr. Sheldon willingly and voluntarily pitted his skill and aircraft against odds. His intrepid feat adds lustre to the memory of those stalwart pilots whose rare courage and indomitable spirit have conquered the vastness of the Alaskan Territory."

This was only one of the many spectacular rescue missions Sheldon would carry out, most of them involving harrowing flights into the mountains he loved so much. On Christmas Day, 1958, he heard from the 10th Rescue Division at Elmendorf Air Force Base in Anchorage that a C-54 transport was missing; the plane carried passengers, holiday mail and the payroll for the Aleutian Sheyma Air Force Base. "Tenth Rescue didn't initiate a search because of the weather," Sheldon recalled, "and the guy asked me if I'd be interested, to which I said, 'You bet!' After I hung up, I looked at the weather south of town, and I knew that this wouldn't be any lark, 'cause she was stacked up like sour biscuit dough as far as I could see, which wasn't very far."

No man to turn back as long as there was a possibility of saving lives, Sheldon loaded some extra cans of fuel into his Super Cub, along with a pair of snowshoes and his red nylon bag stuffed with survival gear, and took off. A hunch—and he was always one to listen to his hunches—told him to go look for the plane in the vicinity of Mount Iliamna, an active 10,016-foot-high volcano lying 180 miles south of Talkeetna. Tenth Rescue had told him that clouds blanketed the volcano, and when Sheldon arrived there, he found that the weather had not changed. "It looked like a milk shake," he said.

Searching for a break in the clouds, Sheldon flew toward Iniskin Bay to the south. "I noticed right off when I got to Iniskin that the wind, which was blasting out of the south, was thinning the cloud deck on that side of the mountain but the north side was a swirling mass of snow, pushed by a wind that I estimated to be blowing at about 30 to 40 knots." Yet it was toward the north side that he headed, impelled by the notion that he would find the plane there. "I got as low as I could after I ducked into the clouds, and like I figured, couldn't see a thing except occasional snow and rocks. I could smell the stinking sulphur fumes from the volcano rifts as I got downwind of 'em, and it was a bad scene. Each time I punched a hole in the low clouds, I hoped they weren't stuffed with rocks."

Now another hunch told him that he ought to be flying higher—that the C-54 was somewhere on the mountain, between 8,500 and 9,000 feet. He began climbing. He had just about made up his mind that he would not be able to get to 9,000 feet "when out of the corner of my eye, I spotted something that made my old ticker stand still." There on the snow below, scattered for a half mile, was the wreckage of a plane. No one could have survived such a crash. Sheldon swerved and came in for another pass in an effort to read the number on the plane's tail. But snow and sulfur fumes limited visibility and he had to make seven passes, at 50 feet of altitude, before he finally got the whole number—which he radioed to 10th Rescue. It was that of the missing transport. Sick at heart, Sheldon flew to the coast and landed in a cove, refueled and headed back for Talkeetna. For his heroic effort, he was awarded another citation—this time by the Air Force.

The story does not quite end. Six years later Sheldon was hired by a man who called himself a prospector to fly to Mount Iliamna; the man said he wanted to search there for ore. Sheldon landed the man and his 2,000-pound load near the peak when he suddenly realized "we were at 8,250 feet, just two miles west of the snow-buried site of the crash."

The site had been declared off limits by the Air Force because the payroll was still there, somewhere in the snow. "My flesh crawled when it dawned on me what this dude had in mind. I walked up to the guy and said, 'If you plan to salvage valuables from that C-54, mister, you're going to do it over my dead body, and you got just 20 more seconds to get your butt into this here Cub, or I'm headed for Elmendorf.'" The treasure seeker got back into the Cub and Sheldon returned him posthaste to Talkeetna.

Adventurers of another sort kept Sheldon busy throughout the summers. Reflecting a postwar resurgence in mountain climbing, teams of alpinists from around the world thronged to Alaska to attack Mount McKinley and other challenging peaks. Each season Sheldon found himself flying at least 100 climbers to and from base camps—and all too often going to the aid of those who got into trouble. He learned to keep a fatherly eye on the climbers as he went about his general aviation chores, watching their antlike progress up the slopes. And he acted quickly whenever he got word that someone was injured or suffering from ailments to which mountaineers are vulnerable—frostbite, oxygen depletion or pulmonary edema, a build-up of fluid in the lungs.

The winds blowing around Mount McKinley—especially the downdrafts that spilled over the ridges like waterfalls—made most landings so tricky that, as fellow bush pilot Pete Haggland put it, they "would raise hair on a frozen orange.'' For work in the mountains, Sheldon used what was then his favorite plane, a yellow Piper Super Cub equipped with a 150-horsepower engine. The added power, combined with the plane's light airframe, made it ideal for maneuvering at high altitudes in the mountains. As soon as retractable skis became available, in 1951, Sheldon installed them on the Super Cub. The skis had slots through which the wheels extended, enabling him to take off from a regular landing strip. Once airborne, he used a lever to lower the skis over the tires, making it possible to land on snow or ice. Constructed of aluminum, they were a vast improvement over the fixed, heavy skis of hardwood and stainless steel used since the days of Bob Reeve.

With his nimble Super Cub and his retractable skis, Sheldon took up a practice that he had found incredible years earlier when he heard that Bob Reeve was doing it: landing on glaciers. Dancing on the tricky air currents above a glacial slope, Sheldon would judge his moment carefully and then roar in for a landing, run up the incline at full power and turn the plane sideways at the top to keep it from sliding backward. Weather permitting, he would fly in and out of the mountains week after week during the climbing season, sometimes making several landings a day. From his Talkeetna airstrip, where the teams of mountaineers camped in his hangar awaiting their turn, Sheldon first ferried in their gear. Then he returned for groups of climbers, always hustling them along with what became his litany, "Let's *go!* We got to *move!*"

Flying with Sheldon spared the teams days of overland travel, conserving vital energy for the main climb, and saved them money by eliminating the need to hire and organize a pack train. In 1953, Sheldon flew one University of California group to Anderson Glacier, jumping-off point for peaks in the Mount Logan-Mount Lucania country. It took 15 trips to transfer the climbers and their gear onto the treacherous ice at about 6,000 feet. That same year he delivered an Austrian-led team to a point just below a fearsome mile-high icefall on the flank of previously unscaled Mount Deborah, 120 miles northeast of Mount McKinley.

The challenges posed by these airlifts were nothing compared with the one that confronted Sheldon in the summer of 1960 when disaster struck on the high crags of mighty Mount McKinley. Four experienced climbers in a team led by John Day, an Oregon rancher in his fifties who was an enthusiastic mountaineer, were picking their way down the ice-glazed granite just below McKinley's summit when one man slipped. As he fell, the length of rope that secured him to the other climbers pulled a second man down. Then the third fell, and the fourth. They clawed at the granite with their ice axes, but nothing could stop their 400-foot slide to a narrow ledge. There they crunched into the packed snow. Two of the men were merely stunned, but the third suffered a concussion and Day was immobilized by torn ligaments in his left leg.

Eight hundred feet below them, a party of mountaineers from Anchorage on the way down the peak heard the men's cries and watched helplessly as the climbers fell. Three of the onlookers started rescaling

Sheldon indicates a turn he is about to make on his way to pluck a party of German climbers from Mount McKinley. For a job like this, he often used one of his two Cessnas, which could carry up to five passengers, but for exploring new landing sites he much preferred the agility of his smaller Piper Super Cubs.

After landing on a snowy slope of Alaska's Ruth Glacier, Don Sheldon swings his plane around for a downhill takeoff. Sheldon described the site, where his hexagonal ski lodge (far right) perched on a crag 100 feet from an outhouse, as "the only place I know where you can step out to the powder room and fall 6,000 feet."

the mountain to help. Coincidentally, 1,000 feet farther down the mountain, another member of the Anchorage group, a woman named Helga Bading, lay in a small tent suffering from oxygen depletion. At first her problem had not seemed serious; some people react more severely than others to the thin air of high altitudes. But later she became incoherent and could not keep food down. Climber Paul Crews turned on an emergency radio transmitter to call for help, not only for Helga Bading, but for the four men above who lay dazed and battered where they had fallen. The call was received by the 10th Rescue Division in Anchorage, which in turn notified Don Sheldon. They recognized that there was no one in Alaska with surer knowledge of Mount McKinley than Sheldon, and feared that their helicopters might not be able to reach the altitudes he could in his plane. Besides, he was a whole lot closer to the accident than they.

Sheldon already knew the two teams of climbers involved. He had flown them to the mountain in the first place. Since then he had checked on their progress from time to time and had an idea of their general location. His first move was to load a few emergency supplies into his Super Cub and take off.

Though the victims were on the South Face of the mountain, Sheldon deliberately headed for the cloud-enveloped North Face, where the wind would be less. Donning an oxygen mask, he rode the updrafts to 19,000 feet. He then flew around to the South Face. Slowly descending through the clouds and wind in a tight spiral, he emerged directly over the accident scene.

He could see where the men had fallen and the tent they had set up for shelter. But about 200 yards away from the climbers Sheldon saw something that made him wince—the smoldering wreckage of a Cessna 180. A pilot named William Stevenson had been flying in the vicinity when curiosity about the events on McKinley led him to take a look. He flew the Cessna too close to the mountain, and in trying to turn sharply away caused the plane to stall. The Cessna crashed and exploded in flame, killing Stevenson and a passenger he was carrying.

Sheldon dropped the emergency supplies to the injured men, put the plane in a spiraling climb and recrossed to the North Face. Clear of the clouds, he headed for the Federal Aviation Agency station at Summit to refuel. There Sheldon found Army helicopters standing by, ready to attempt a rescue of their own. He offered to guide the pilots to the accident site, but they declined, saying that the choppers would be too fast for the Cub. As it turned out, neither helicopter made it. One developed electrical problems and had to turn back, and the other got lost in fog. Sheldon now undertook to ferry rescue teams to the lower slopes. By the second day, he had hauled five teams to Mount McKinley.

He had hardly returned from the last ferry flight when word arrived by radio that Helga Bading would be doomed unless she was brought down soon. Sheldon was asked to attempt a landing on the mountain at 14,000 feet. The other members of Helga Bading's party could lower

the woman that far on a fiberglass sled that had been airdropped to them. Aware of the risks, he agreed to try. It would be the first time anyone had set down so high on the mountain.

Sheldon spoke by telephone with the one man who knew Mount McKinley even more intimately than he did—Boston scientist and mountaineer Bradford Washburn. Studying his collection of photographs of McKinley in his Boston office, Washburn spotted a small slope near a feature of the mountain known as the West Buttress where a landing just might be possible. It was a short, perilous shelflike basin of crusted snow, slanted at a frightening angle. Washburn gave Sheldon the landmarks he would need to find it.

Though landing on such a spot posed grave difficulties, a successful takeoff was chancy in the extreme. At that altitude, the engine of Sheldon's plane produced 45 per cent less power than at sea level. In order to become airborne with Helga Bading aboard, he would have to go in light, carrying only minimal survival gear and no more fuel than absolutely necessary to make the pickup and return to Talkeetna.

Sheldon took off early the next morning, accompanied, in another Super Cub, by Anchorage pilot George Kitchen, who had come along to lend a hand if needed. They soon found the landing site Washburn had selected. "The spot looked mighty small and had a brisk slope," Sheldon later said. The snowy patch, which was no more than 2,000 feet long, ended abruptly in a rock wall that reared upward to McKinley's North Summit. At the lower end, the slope was slashed with frightening crevasses, then ended in a sheer cliff.

Holding his breath, he made his approach at full power to guarantee that he would not stop dead after landing on the slope, and headed for the snow crust just above the lower brink. "I knew," Sheldon recalled, "I had to get every available inch out of the landing surface or risk spreading my airplane and myself all over the side of McKinley." And once into a landing, Sheldon had to go through with it; the mountain terrain would not let him go around for a second try. At just the right second he pulled the plane's nose up, touched down the skis, then drove up the slope straight for the rock face. As he neared it, he abruptly swung the tail around and put the throttle to idle. The plane was now fixed in position, at a right angle to the incline. Sheldon and six climbers from other expeditions that happened also to be on the mountain spent the next hour packing the snow to make an airstrip while George Kitchen circled above. Sheldon then marked it with bright orange tape stretched between willow sticks he had brought along for the purpose.

Now it was Kitchen's turn to land. He was an expert flying instructor and Sheldon would try to talk him in. On the radio, Sheldon reminded Kitchen to come in at full power. But Kitchen involuntarily followed the flier's ingrained habit of throttling back as he touched down on the slope. The plane lost its forward momentum and, for a moment, seemed as though it might slide backward into space. Kitchen frantically revved the engine to full power again and the skis held on the crust—

In an attempt to reach climbers stranded high on Mount McKinley in June 1960, two members of a rescue team set out from their base camp 10,200 feet up the mountain's flank. The relief parties and their gear had been flown to the site by Don Sheldon, whose Piper Super Cub rests nearby.

right in the middle of the airstrip. Somehow, that second Super Cub had to be maneuvered up the slope so that it could be turned for takeoff.

While Kitchen kept up full power, the six climbers joined Sheldon in shoving Kitchen's Super Cub up the slope. The task took an exhausting three hours. By then Helga Bading, distinctly blue from lack of oxygen, had been brought down on the fiberglass sled. When they had packed her aboard Sheldon's Cub, he turned the plane around and fire-walled the throttle. If he did not achieve takeoff speed quickly, he would plunge into one of the crevasses dead ahead. The plane roared down the shelf. The tail lifted and then, just as Sheldon came to the last of the field markers he had set out, the Cub floated into the air.

Now it was helicopter pilot Link Luckett's turn to perform an astonishing feat of flying. When the Cub touched down at Talkeetna with Helga Bading—who was quickly moved to an Air Force transport and taken to Anchorage—Sheldon found Luckett there waiting. Luckett flew for the Hughes Helicopter Service in Anchorage and had brought one of the company's two-place Hiller choppers. The injured men were still up on McKinley, and he was determined to help bring them down, even though they were far above the helicopter's normal ceiling. He had stripped the machine of all unnecessary weight, and he felt he could reach the climbers, but he wanted Sheldon on hand in the Piper Cub.

The two men flew together toward the West Buttress. Aided by thermals, Sheldon climbed relatively quickly to 17,500 feet, just below the ledge where the four men from the John Day party had fallen, then orbited there while Luckett struggled to lift the Hiller above its 16,000-foot operating ceiling, with the throttle pushed to the stops. In what seemed like an eternity to Sheldon, the chopper made it and Luckett settled it down close to Day's camp, establishing an altitude record for the Hiller. He discovered that two of the climbers were now sufficiently recovered to make their own way down the mountain, but that Day's leg and the other climber's concussion were so disabling that the two men would have to be lifted out. Luckett took off with Day first, ferrying him down to the packed-snow airstrip Sheldon had taken off from with Helga Bading. Luckett then returned to the ledge a second time to pick up the other climber and bring him down. The two other mountaineers who had been well enough to make the descent on their own had already arrived. Now Sheldon relayed the four down to a fairly flat portion of the mountainside at 10,200 feet, where waiting military and civilian aircraft carried them to safety.

In the valley below, when the rescue work was over, the helicopter pilot and the bush pilot were given a hero's welcome. But Sheldon's work was not finished. Although he had snatched only a short nap or two in the preceding four days and had eaten little, he insisted on flying back to Mount McKinley. He had flown in several rescue teams, and feeling responsible for their safety, he could not leave them there. So he made another 18 trips before finally consenting to eat and sleep. Sheldon's contribution to the rescue operation was heralded as

Sheldon and chopper pilot Link Luckett fly toward Mount McKinley during the 1960 mission on which Luckett rescued two injured climbers.

"one of the most daredevil feats in the long history of Alaskan aviation."

Since the death of his partner, Stub Morrison, Sheldon had run the Talkeetna Air Service pretty much by himself. But in 1964, four years after the Mount McKinley drama, Sheldon married and got a new partner. She was Roberta Reeve, daughter of Bob Reeve, the original glacier pilot. The couple flew to a remote cabin on the shore of a frozen lake for their honeymoon. During the night a warm wind softened the ice, and the plane, which the groom had left parked on its surface, plunged through. Don was obliged to radio for help, sheepishly asking his colleagues to wing in and help him retrieve his plane from the water.

Lakes, in fact, seemed to be Sheldon's principal nemesis, becoming the watery graveyards of several of his planes. The lake where he had crashed with Frank Moennikes he named Eight Grand Lake because that was the value of the aircraft he lost there. "There's a Twenty-six-and-a-half Grand Lake, too," he would tell friends. "But I don't even like to think about that one."

In all, Sheldon smashed up six aircraft in the course of flying more

Roberta Sheldon embraces her husband, safely home from another day's work. It was Roberta who kept the couple's Talkeetna Air Service running efficiently—serving as business manager, booking agent and radio dispatcher while Don did the flying.

than a million miles, but he never lost a passenger. When he died in 1975 at the age of 53 it was not in the cockpit but in bed, with Roberta sitting at his side. And it was not flying that killed him. Nor was the wilderness to blame. Don Sheldon succumbed to cancer.

"The hours are too long," Sheldon had once said, summing up his career, "and the pay's not good enough. If you make it, everybody says, hooray! But when you don't, you shouldn't have been doing the damn stunt anyway. But whoopee, boy," he would explode, "you just can't sit around like a vegetable. You got to *do* something!"

Sheldon could have been speaking for all bush pilots, for men blessed as he was with inexhaustible energy and an unquenchable passion for flying. Attracted to peril and uncertainty, they reveled in the excitement of aviation in Godforsaken corners of the world. Few were saints, yet many of them selflessly put themselves in mortal danger for little more reward than a handshake or a heartfelt expression of gratitude. And they were businessmen, however casual, whose wherewithal to continue flying depended almost solely upon their willingness to labor long and hard, often under miserable conditions. A successful few transcended this mean existence and became the proprietors of companies that grew until they had as much in common with conventional airlines as they did with bush-flying services.

But the bush pilots were more than adventurers and entrepreneurs; they made possible things that might never have happened, or that would have occurred much later without them. Graziers in Australia's great Outback might still be living for the most part without wives had it not been for aviators such as Norman Brearley and Hudson Fysh. Thousands of people would have lost their lives in Australia and elsewhere had there not been bush pilots to bring help or carry the sick and injured to hospitals. Without such men as Battling Ray Parer and Pard Mustar, New Guinea's mountain gold fields would have lain untapped for perhaps another decade. And Angel Fall? It would no doubt have been discovered sooner or later, but never more engagingly than by the man who searched so long and fruitlessly for the gold on Devil Mountain.

By the early 1980s the heyday of the bush pilot had passed. Gone was the time when he could run a one-man show and keep his records in a notebook in his pocket; government regulations had heaped an ever-increasing burden of paper work on the lone operator. In Alaska the annual cost of insurance on a plane—about 8 per cent of its value—could range from $3,600 on up; liability insurance could run almost $1,000 per passenger seat each year.

Civilization had taken root in many of the places where the bush pilots once flew alone, and there, as often as not, a large company or a government provided air services. Still, the chances are that where true wilderness survives, nearby will be a pioneering pilot ready and eager to be of assistance—and to tell a few good yarns in the bargain.

A twin-engined Beechcraft cruises above Alaska's Herbert Glacier after dropping off a party of kayakers on Berners Bay, northwest of Juneau.

Acknowledgments

The index for this book was prepared by Gale Linck Partoyan. For their valuable help in the preparation of this volume, the editors thank: **In Australia:** New South Wales—Miss J. Ball, Qantas Airways; Jack Treacey; Queensland—Colonel Kelly; Bernard Parer; Royal Flying Doctor Service; James Sinclair; Western Australia—Sir Norman Brearley. **In Canada:** Manitoba—Gordon Emberley, Executive Director, Western Canada Aviation Museum; Ontario—R. W. Bradford, Curator, Aviation and Space Division, National Museum of Science and Technology; Guy Jessier, Peter Robertson, National Photographic Collection. **In France:** Paris—Général Pierre Lissarague, Director, Général Roger de Ruffray, Deputy-Director, Colonel Pierre Willefert, Curator, Musée de l'Air; Colonel Edmond Petit, Curator, Musée Air-France. **In Mexico:** Chihuahua—Captain Leo Lopez Talamantes, Servicio Aereo Lopez, S.A. **In the United States:** Alaska—James Greiner; Roberta Sheldon; Nancy Turner, Reeve Aleutian Airways; California—Marie Angel; Gordon Barry; Langan Swent; Washington, D.C.—Jerry Hannifin, Aeronautics Correspondent, *Time;* Patricia Kay, Australian Embassy; Donald S. Lopez, Karl Schneidi, National Air and Space Museum; Philip Schleib; Florida—Elaine Harrison; Maryland—Theron K. Rinehart, Fairchild Republic Company; Edward Slattery; Virginia—Russell Sackett; Washington—Lloyd Jarman; Kate Kennedy; Pat Mills. **In West Germany:** Munich—Walter Zucker.

Bibliography

Books

Affleck, Arthur H., *The Wandering Years.* Croyden: Longmans, 1964.

Allen, Richard Sanders, *Revolution in the Sky: Those Fabulous Lockheeds, the Pilots Who Flew Them.* The Stephen Greene Press, 1964.

Angel, Marie, *The Angel Falls.* Unpublished manuscript.

Angelucci, Enzo, and Paolo Matricardi, *World Aircraft 1918-1935.* Rand McNally & Company, 1979.

Bowers, Peter, *Yesterday's Wings.* Aircraft Owners and Pilots Association, 1974.

Brearley, Norman, with Ted Mayman, *Australian Aviator.* Adelaide: Rigby Limited, 1971.

Copley, Greg, *Australians in the Air.* Adelaide: Rigby Limited, 1976.

Davies, R.E.G.:
Airlines of Latin America since 1919. London: Putnam, 1983.
A History of the World's Airlines. London: Oxford University Press, 1964.

Day, Beth, *Glacier Pilot: The Story of Bob Reeve and the Flyers Who Pushed Back Alaska's Air Frontiers.* Holt, Rinehart and Winston, 1957.

Dennison, L. R., *Devil Mountain.* Hastings House, 1942.

Dwiggins, Don, *The Barnstormers: Flying Daredevils of the Roaring Twenties.* Grosset & Dunlap, 1968.

Elliot, Elisabeth, *Through Gates of Splendour.* London: Hodder & Stoughton, 1957.

Ellis, Frank H., *Canada's Flying Heritage.* Toronto: University of Toronto Press, 1954.

Ellison, Norman, *Flying Matilda: Early Days in Australian Aviation.* Sydney: Angus and Robertson, 1957.

Fysh, Hudson, *Qantas Rising: The Autobiography of the Flying Fysh.* Sydney: Angus and Robertson, 1965.

Gibbs-Smith, Charles Harvard, *Aviation: An Historical Survey from its Origins to the End of World War II.* London: Her Majesty's Stationery Office, 1970.

Gleason, Robert J., *Icebound in the Siberian Arctic.* Alaska Northwest Publishing, 1977.

Godwin, John, *Battling Parer.* Adelaide: Rigby Limited, 1968.

Greiner, James, *Wager with the Wind: The Don Sheldon Story.* Rand McNally & Company, 1974.

Gwynn-Jones, Terry:
Heroic Australian Air Stories. Adelaide: Rigby Limited, 1981.
True Australian Air Stories. Adelaide: Rigby Limited, 1977.

Harkey, Ira, *Pioneer Bush Pilot: The Story of Noel Wien.* University of Washington Press, 1974.

Helmericks, Harmon, *The Last of the Bush Pilots.* Alfred A. Knopf, 1970.

Hitt, Russell T., *Jungle Pilot: The Life and Witness of Nate Saint.* Harper & Brothers, 1959.

Ingells, Douglas J., with Ralph Dietrick, *Tin Goose: The Fabulous Ford Trimotor.* Aero Publishers, Inc., 1968.

Jackson, A. J., *De Havilland Aircraft since 1909.* London: Putnam, 1962.

Keith, Ronald A., *Bush Pilot with a Briefcase: The Happy-Go-Lucky Story of Grant McConachie.* Doubleday & Company, Inc., 1972.

Lewis, Peter:
The British Bomber since 1914: Fifty Years of Design and Development. London: Putnam, 1967.
The British Fighter since 1912: Sixty-seven Years of Design and Development. London: Putnam, 1979.

Miller, Robin, *Flying Nurse.* Taplinger Publishing Company, 1972.

Mills, Stephen E., and James W. Phillips, *Sourdough Sky: A Pictorial History of Flights and Flyers in the Bush Country.* Superior Publishing Company, 1969.

Molson, K. M., *Pioneering in Canadian Air Transport.* Winnipeg: James Richardson & Sons, Limited, 1942.

Parsons, H. P., *Trail of the Wild Goose.* Dryden, Ontario: Alex Wilson Publications Limited, 1978.

Potter, Jean, *Flying Frontiersmen.* The Macmillan Company, 1956.

Rhys, Lloyd, *High Lights and Flights in New Guinea.* London: Hodder and Stoughton Limited, 1942.

Satterfield, Archie, *In the Float Country.* Bonanza Books, 1969.

Sinclair, James:
Sepik Pilot: Wing Commander Bobby Gibbes. Melbourne: Lansdowne, 1971.
Wings of Gold: How the Aeroplane Developed New Guinea. Sydney: Pacific Publications, 1978.

Schleit, Philip, *Shelton's Barefoot Airlines.* Fishergate Publishing Company, Inc., 1982.

Shaw, Margaret Mason, *Bush Pilots: Canadian Portraits.* Toronto: Clarke, Irwin & Company Limited, 1962.

Turner, P. St. John, *Pictorial History of Pan American World Airways.* London: Ian Allan, 1973.

Wagner, William, *Ryan Broughams and Their Builders.* Historical Aviation Album, 1974.

Weiss, David Ansel, *The Saga of the Tin Goose.* Crown Publishers, Inc., 1971.

Periodicals

Champlin, Charles, "Intrepid Men vs. Mighty Mac: Magnificent Rescue on McKinley." *Life,* June 6, 1960.

Deutsch, Hermann B., "Flying the Jungle Run." *The Saturday Evening Post,* December 3, 1938.

Elliot, Elisabeth, and staff reporters of *Life,* "Child Among Her Father's Killers; Missionaries Live with Aucas." *Life,* November 24, 1958.
" 'Go Ye and Preach the Gospel.' " *Life,* January 30, 1956.

Moser, Donald, "A Bush Pilot's Deadly, Daily Game." *Life,* November 27, 1964.

Mydans, Carl, "The Bush Pilot of Angel Falls." *Life,* October 15, 1965.

"Planes for the Jungle Hops." *Fortune,* April 1945.

Scullin, George, "The Flying Hobo." *Cavalier,* March 1959.

Picture credits

The sources for the illustrations in this book are listed below. Credits from left to right are separated by semicolons; from top to bottom they are separated by dashes.
Endpaper (and cover detail, regular edition): Painting by Frank Wootton. 6, 7: Denny Hewitt, courtesy R. W. Stevens Collection. 8: Courtesy K. M. Molson. 9: A. A. Koch, from *Wings of Gold* by James Sinclair, published by Pacific Publishers, Sydney and New York, 1978. 10, 11: Langan W. Swent. 12, 13: Lloyd R. Jarman. 14, 15: From *The Australian Aviator* by Sir Norman Brearley, published by Rigby Publishers, Australia, 1971. 16, 17: © Cornell Capa/Magnum. 18: R. W. Stevens Collection. 21-24: National Aeronautical Collection, Ottawa, Neg. Nos. 2703, 1491, 2278 and 8488. 25-28: Public Archives of Canada, Neg. Nos. 89694, C65260 and 89806. 29, 31: Courtesy K. M. Molson. 32: Gordon W. Werne, courtesy Jesse Davidson Aviation History Archives—R. W. Stevens Collection. 33: National Aeronautical Collection, Ottawa, Neg. No. 6354—Gordon W. Werne, courtesy Jesse Davidson Aviation History Archives. 35: R. W. Stevens Collection. 36: Courtesy K. M. Molson; from *Bush Pilot with a Briefcase* by Ronald A. Keith, published by Doubleday and Company, New York, 1972—Public Archives of Canada, Neg. No. C65272. 37: Public Archives of Canada, Neg. Nos. C62081, C63301 and C23486. 38, 39: University of Alaska, Noel Wien Collection. 40: Wide World. 43: Map by Jaime Quintero—Lillian Crosson Frizell Collection. 44, 45: Robert J. Gleason, from *Icebound in the Siberian Arctic* by Robert J. Gleason, published by Alaska Northwest Publishing Company, Anchorage, 1977—Lillian Crosson Frizell Collection (2). 46: Lillian Crosson Frizell Collection. 49: Russ Dow, courtesy Bob Reeve Collection—courtesy Bob Reeve Collection. 50: Bradford Washburn, courtesy Bob Reeve Collection. 51: Russ Dow, courtesy Bob Reeve Collection. 52, 53: Courtesy Bob Reeve Collection. 54, 55: Public Archives of Canada, Neg. No. C65258. 56, 57: Courtesy K. M. Molson. 58-63: Public Archives of Canada, Neg. Nos. C65244, A88683 and C57532. 64, 67: Gwynn-Jones Collection. 68: Qantas Airways Ltd., courtesy Gwynn-Jones Collection. 69: Qantas Airways Ltd. 71: Gwynn-Jones Collection. 72-74: West Australian Newspapers, Ltd. 75: Map by Jaime Quintero. 77, 78: Qantas Airways Ltd. 79: Royal Flying Doctor Service, Western Australia, courtesy Gwynn-Jones Collection. 80: Royal Flying Doctor Service, Western Australia. 82, 83: Qantas Airways, Ltd. 84, 85: From *The Australian Aviator* by Sir Norman Brearley, published by Rigby Publishers, Australia, 1971. 87-89: Gwynn-Jones Collection. 90, 91: H. L. Downing, from *Wings of Gold* by James Sinclair. 92: Gwynn-Jones Collection. 93: Map by Jaime Quintero. 96-99: Ian Grabowsky, from *Wings of Gold* by James Sinclair. 100: Keith Alderson, from *Wings of Gold* by James Sinclair. 102: Charles Marshall, from *Wings of Gold* by James Sinclair. 103: Gwynn-Jones Collection. 104: A. A. Koch, from *Wings of Gold* by James Sinclair. 109: © Cornell Capa/Mag- num. 110, 111: A. A. Koch, from *Wings of Gold* by James Sinclair. 112, 113: Ian Grabowsky, from *Wings of Gold* by James Sinclair (2); R. O. Mant, from *Wings of Gold* by James Sinclair. 114, 115: Timothy G. Wright, from *Wings of Gold* by James Sinclair, inset, from *High Lights and Flights in New Guinea, 1942* by Lloyd Rhys, published by Hodder and Stoughton, Ltd., Australia, 1942. 116, 117: Langan W. Swent. 122: Philip W. Payne. 123: Carl Mydans for *Life*. 124: Jimmie Angel, courtesy Marie Angel. 125: Gustavo Heny, courtesy Time, Inc. Picture Collection. 128-131: Langan W. Swent. 133: Courtesy Leo Lopez. 134: From *Jungle Pilot* by Russell T. Hitt. Copyright © 1959 by The Auca Missionary Foundation. Reprinted by permission of Harper and Row Publishers, Inc. 136: Nate Saint; from *Jungle Pilot* by Russell T. Hitt. Copyright © 1959 by The Auca Missionary Foundation. Reprinted by permission of Harper and Row Publishers, Inc.; Nate Saint (5). 137: © Cornell Capa/Magnum. 138: From *Through Gates of Splendor* by Elisabeth Elliot, published by Harper and Row, 1957. 140, 141: © Cornell Capa/Magnum, inset, Major Malcolm L. Nurnberg. 142-149: Artwork by John Batchelor. 150, 151: Courtesy Sheldon Family Collection. 153: Carl Shatto, courtesy Sheldon Family Collection. 156: Lee Friedlander, courtesy Sheldon Family Collection. 160, 161: N. R. Farbman for *Life*. 162, 163: Dale M. Brown. 164: Grey Villet for *Life*. 166, 167: Harriss Darby for the Anchorage *Times*. 168: N. R. Farbman for *Life*. 170, 171: Kit Kittle.

Index